# ALSO BY CLARENCE TALLEY SR.

*The Call for the Prophet*

*A Call from God*

*Is It True: Reflections from the Word of God*

*Lie after Lie after Lie: A Study in 2 Kings 5*

*God in the Land of Ghana: He's Everywhere*

*Jesus Christ Made Straight A's*

*From the Pulpit to the Streets*

*Cruising with Jonah*

# Seven Things God Hates

*A Biblical Perspective on Righteous Hate*

DR. CLARENCE TALLEY SR.

Copyright © 2018 Dr. Clarence Talley Sr..

All rights reserved. No part of this book may be used or reproduced by any means, graphic, electronic, or mechanical, including photocopying, recording, taping or by any information storage retrieval system without the written permission of the author except in the case of brief quotations embodied in critical articles and reviews.

Scripture taken from the King James Version of the Bible.

THE HOLY BIBLE, NEW INTERNATIONAL VERSION®, NIV® Copyright © 1973, 1978, 1984, 2011 by Biblica, Inc.® Used by permission. All rights reserved worldwide.

Scripture quotations marked (NLT) are taken from the Holy Bible, New Living Translation, copyright © 1996, 2004, 2007 by Tyndale House Foundation. Used by permission of Tyndale House Publishers, Inc., Carol Stream, Illinois 60188. All rights reserved.

Scripture taken from the NEW AMERICAN STANDARD BIBLE®, Copyright © 1960, 1962, 1963, 1968, 1971, 1972, 1973, 1975, 1977, 1995 by The Lockman Foundation. Used by permission.

This book is a work of non-fiction. Unless otherwise noted, the author and the publisher make no explicit guarantees as to the accuracy of the information contained in this book and in some cases, names of people and places have been altered to protect their privacy.

WestBow Press books may be ordered through booksellers or by contacting:

WestBow Press
A Division of Thomas Nelson & Zondervan
1663 Liberty Drive
Bloomington, IN 47403
www.westbowpress.com
1 (866) 928-1240

Because of the dynamic nature of the Internet, any web addresses or links contained in this book may have changed since publication and may no longer be valid. The views expressed in this work are solely those of the author and do not necessarily reflect the views of the publisher, and the publisher hereby disclaims any responsibility for them.

Any people depicted in stock imagery provided by Getty Images are models, and such images are being used for illustrative purposes only.
Certain stock imagery © Getty Images.

ISBN: 978-1-9736-2849-1 (sc)
ISBN: 978-1-9736-2939-9 (hc)
ISBN: 978-1-9736-2850-7 (e)

Library of Congress Control Number: 2018905766

Print information available on the last page.

WestBow Press rev. date: 05/29/2018

# CONTENTS

Preface .................................................................. ix
Introduction ........................................................... xi

1   Hate Defined ...................................................... 1
2   A Proud Look .................................................... 9
3   A Lying Tongue ................................................ 21
4   Hands That Shed Innocent Blood ...................... 34
5   A Heart That Devises Wicked Imaginations ...... 45
6   Feet That Be Swift in Running to Mischief ....... 56
7   A False Witness That Speaketh Lies ................. 66
8   He That Soweth Discord among the Brethren ..... 76

Concluding Thoughts ............................................. 83
Appendix 1   Forty-Three Things God Hates ........... 87
Appendix 2   Jesus Christ's Use of the Word Hate ..... 91
Bibliography ......................................................... 93

To
The Mount

Seekers of Truth—Lovers of God

# PREFACE

This book is not about hate crimes. It is not primarily about hate as experienced by humankind. It is about sin. It is about love. This book is about what the great God of the universe hates and why. It is a look at seven specific sins that are repugnant to God and that should also be repugnant to His followers.

Acts of hatred invade our lives from many sources. We are inundated with violent acts, many of which are motivated by hatred. Centuries ago, through the wise Solomon, God clearly set forth seven things that He hates.

God hates anything and anyone that is contrary to His nature. On the other hand, as a God of love, He also loves everyone and requires His followers to do the same. To truly know God is to love God. To truly love God is to hate the things God hates.

The Bible reveals, with specificity, many things that God hates. It is a book that tells us about God, about ourselves, and about the plans and purpose God has for our lives. There's no other source that is perfectly designed to do so.

A focus on the narrow window of Proverbs 6:16–19 presents a panoramic view of God that is often overlooked. Through this narrow window, God reveals a side of Himself that few people take time to consider. As you will see, this lesser-observed perspective, like God's love, permeates the pages of scripture.

In this study of seven things that God hates, it is my hope and prayer that you will draw closer to the God of love and better understand the things He hates.

# INTRODUCTION

In even a casual reading of the Bible, you will discover that God is not only a God who loves but also a God who hates. Just as *divine love* permeates the pages of scripture, so does *divine hatred*—divine hatred for evil and evildoers who act contrary to the will of God. The Bible states emphatically that "God is love" (1 John 4:8), but He is also a God who has a holy abhorrence for both sin and specific sinners whose sins are an abomination in His sight.

It is a biblical fact that God is love, and He loves us—humankind—the crown of His creation (1 John 4:16). Love is God's very nature. It is not simply that the God of the Bible loves us; it must be understood that He is love. God's love flows out of His sovereign will, as does His abhorrence for evil.

> God's love flows out of His sovereign will, as does His abhorrence for evil.

Moses declared the will of God based on His sovereign purpose and love for Israel and for all nations when he said, "The Lord did not set his love upon you, nor choose you because ye were more in number than any other people; for ye were the fewest of all people; but because the Lord loved thee" (Deuteronomy 7:7–8). The apostle Paul, writing to the Christians at Rome and to all New Testament believers, proclaimed God's will and all-encompassing love when he said,

"But God commendeth his love toward us, in that, while we were yet sinners, Christ died for us" (Romans 5:8).

From the opening pages of the Bible, we see the love of God at work. There, we hear God speaking words of creativity—"Let there be"—to an earth He was making habitable for man. God created man to reflect His image, rule creation, produce godly offspring, and most importantly, fellowship with man forever (Genesis 1–2).

And in the closing pages of the Bible, we see a God who is readying to "come quickly" and restore humankind to the loving relationship so desperately sought after throughout human history (Revelation 22). From Genesis to the close of Revelation, God's love is poured out on humankind.

As a result, scripture is replete with examples of God's love, a love that is described in numerous ways. Jeremiah 31:3 speaks of an everlasting love: "I have loved you with an everlasting love; I have drawn you with loving-kindness." Romans 5:5 expresses a sacrificial love: "For we know how dearly God loves us, because he has given us the Holy Spirit to fill our hearts with his love." Romans 8:35–39 describes a love that, though challenged by formidable forces—tribulation, distress, persecution—remains unbreakable and inseparable: "Nothing shall be able to separate us from the love of God, which is in Christ Jesus our Lord."

Ephesians 2:4–5 calls God's love great, a love that makes us alive with Jesus Christ. Ephesians 3:18 labels God's love as immeasurable and incomprehensible, and in John 13:34–35, we are commanded to love others; in doing so, believers are identified with Jesus Christ: "By this shall all men know that you are my disciples, if you love one another" (NIV). One would be hard-pressed to miss the magnificent fact of God's love as expressed in both the Old and New Testaments.

When Jesus Christ was asked by a lawyer, "Master, which is the great commandment in the law?" (Matthew 22:35), Jesus responded by quoting two Old Testament scriptures that command love. The Master stated, "Thou shalt love the Lord thy God with all thy heart, and with all thy soul, and with all thy mind. This is the first and great commandment. And the second is like unto it, Thou shalt love thy neighbor as thyself. On these two commandments hang all the law and the prophets" (Matthew 22:37–40, quoting Deuteronomy 6:5 and Leviticus 19:18, respectively). The great command of scripture is to love— to love God, to love self, and to love one's neighbor.

God's love is a reoccurring theme in the teaching, preaching, and praise ministries of the church. Most churchgoers particularly remember singing "Jesus Loves Me" as children.

> Jesus loves me this I know,
> For the Bible tells me so.
> Little ones to Him belong;
> They are weak, but He is strong.
> Yes, Jesus loves me.

Other songs such as "Love Lifted Me," "Jesus Loves the Little Children," "There Is No Greater Love," and many other great love songs of the church celebrate the fact that God is a God of love (*The New National Baptist Hymnal* 1982).

The whole thrust of the Old and New Testaments hinges on the love of God for man and His disdain for sin. The epitome of

> The great command of scripture is to love—to love God, to love self, and to love one's neighbor.

> The epitome of God's love for man is seen in the person of Jesus Christ, the gift of God to humankind.

xiii

God's love for man is seen in the person of Jesus Christ, the gift of God to humankind. John 3:16 expresses the essence of that love for man: "For God so loved the world that he gave his only begotten Son, that whosoever believeth in him should not perish, but have everlasting life." Love is the scarlet thread of the sacred writings. It is an obvious fact that cannot be easily denied.

> God's holy contempt for sin surpasses human understanding.

Yet God's hatred for evil and wickedness is also evident. It is an often-ignored characteristic of the Lord but a divine characteristic nonetheless. Basic theology teaches that God hates religiosity. In Isaiah 1:13–14, God states His disdain for such practices: "Stop bringing meaningless offerings! Your incense is detestable to me. New Moons, Sabbaths and convocations—I cannot bear your worthless assemblies. Your New Moon feasts and your appointed festivals I hate with all my being." Again, in Amos 5:21, the Lord says, "I hate, I despise your religious festivals; your assemblies are a stench to me." God was fed up with Israel's pretentious worship and their evil scheming against each other (Zechariah 8:17). To these activities, God says, "I hate."

> God is a God of love, but juxtaposed to the love of God is His hatred for those things that are opposed to Him.

The theme of hate, like love, is expressed in the Bible numerous times and in numerous ways: men's hatred toward one another, hatred of the ungodly by the righteous, hatred of the righteous by the ungodly, God's hatred of evil, and the wicked's hatred of God.

God's holy contempt for sin surpasses human understanding.

xiv

God made this clear when He said, "For my thoughts are not your thoughts, neither are your ways my ways. For as the heavens are higher than the earth, so are my ways higher than your ways, and my thoughts than your thoughts" (Isaiah 55:8–9). It is impossible for God to ignore sin or leave it unabated. God opposes sin no matter the form, fashion, or disguise in which it rears its ugly head. His very nature, often described as *holy* and *just*, does not allow Him to compromise with sin. God is a God of love, but juxtaposed to the love of God is His hatred for those things that are opposed to Him.

In this study, we will examine seven particular things God hates that are expressed in Proverbs 6:16–19 and further elucidated throughout scripture. The seven are pride, lying, murder, a bad heart, ungodly feet, perjury, and being a peace-breaker. Throughout this commentary, you will find many inserted scriptures, making it easier to rightfully divide the Word by interpreting scripture with scripture. While I have drawn from numerous translations, the King James Version (KJV) is my primary text. When other versions are used, I have cited them.

First, in chapter 1, we will define the term *hate* and study the term in its various forms, both textually and contextually, as presented in the Old and New Testaments. Next, in each chapter that follows, a detailed analysis of one of the seven items named above that God hates will be presented.

In chapter 2, we will search out the meaning of a *proud look*. It is the first thing God says that He hates. A proud look describes an arrogant soul and a stubborn spirit. Pride is believed to be foundational to all evils and indicative of rebellion against God.

In chapter 3, we will study a *lying tongue* and other elements that are akin to it. The tongue is one of the smallest organs in the body, but it can be used to pervert truth, deceive, and deny godliness.

In chapter 4, we will study the unlawful killing of one person by another—spoken of as *hands that shed innocent blood.* Murder, as it is also known, is the first crime recorded in the Bible. We will learn that it is no trifling matter.

xv

In chapter 5, we will investigate the central organ, the heart—a heart that is not aligned with God, *a heart that deviseth wicked schemes* against others. The heart is identified as the staging point of all actions. It prompts other members of the body to act.

In chapter 6, we will discuss feet that are anxious to carry out the desires of a bad heart. They are described as *feet that run rapidly to evil*. We shall explore the ungodly directions feet are inclined to travel.

In chapter 7, we again will look at the tongue but this time as a tool that bears false witness; in other words, *a false witness who pours out lies*. We shall see how the perversion of truth aimed at hurting others has become "no big deal."

And in chapter 8, where we discuss the last of the seven things God hates, we have a warning against *those who stir up trouble among believers*, rather than seeking to promote peace. Such behavior disgusts God, and He has promised to judge such individuals. Sadly, they will not inherit the kingdom of God.

Finally, if you, the reader, and I, the author, allow the Word of God to speak, we will gain, through this study, a greater understanding of God's contempt for sin and, more specifically, for seven sins that so easily plague and haunt us.

We also will discover that as believers, we are to hate the things God hates, but we are never commanded to hate absolutely or maliciously. Yes, we are to shun evil, to walk lovingly, and to do justly. But most importantly, we must never forget that only God can hate perfectly and love perfectly. I hope this book will help us truly love what God loves and hate the things God hates. Additionally, study questions are included. They are designed to reinforce what you have studied and learned. The questions are laid out in a sequential and systematic way. With holy inspiration, let's begin our journey.

> Only God can hate perfectly and love perfectly.

## Study Questions

1. How can God be a God of love and a God who hates?

2. List scriptures that identify God as a God of love.

3. Using Genesis 1 and 2, explain how God's love is demonstrated.

4. List scriptures that describe God's love.

5. What is the great command of scripture?

6. What is your favorite love song of the church?

7. How is the epitome of God's love confirmed in John 3:16?

8. In what ways is the theme of hate expressed in the Bible?

9. Explain: God's holy contempt for sin surpasses human understanding.

10. List the seven things discussed in this study that God hates.

11. What is your interpretation of the phrase, "Only God can hate perfectly and love perfectly"?

# 1

# HATE DEFINED

The word *hate* is used to express a deep-seated emotion, whether that feeling is toward a person, situation, or thing. Oftentimes, it is used freely to express one's attitude concerning a variety of daily predicaments. Consider the following statements: "I hate him"; "I hate her"; "I hate going to work"; "I hate going to school"; "I hate homework"; "I hate cleaning my room"; "I hate broccoli"; "I hate going to church." There are even those who have said "I hate God."

When I hear others say "I hate ...," I am inclined to respond by saying, "Hate is a very strong word. Surely you do not hate this person, circumstance, or thing. Maybe *dislike* is a better word. Doesn't *dislike* sound less aggressive, less hostile, and less explosive?" More often than not, we all have used the word *hate* to express ourselves literally and hyperbolically.

What, then, does the word *hate* mean? According to *Nelson's Illustrated Bible Dictionary*, the word *hate* or *hatred* is a "strong dislike, disregard, or even indifference toward someone or something; as such, hate may be seated in a person's emotions or will" (Lockyer 1986, 463). *Webster's Dictionary* defines *hate* as "to feel extreme enmity toward: to have a strong aversion to: to find distasteful: to express or feel extreme enmity or active hostility" (1972, 381). In addition, *The Encyclopedia of Biblical Ethics* concludes that *hate* is a "complex reaction" that includes

1

*Dr. Clarence Talley Sr.*

a variety of emotions brought about by individuals and or events (Harrison 1992, 174).

Hate, like love, is often difficult for many to explain or even define in absolute terms. Without a practical definition, both can be used improperly, thereby causing harm to self and others. *Both love and hate can be used constructively and destructively.* For a godly perspective on what is to be believed about a strong negative emotion or dislike, a search of the scriptures is necessary.

Through a search of the Word of God, greater insight and answers to a number of questions about these emotions can be gained. Is hate an emotion the Christian can do without? What does it really mean to hate? What does the Bible teach about hate and hatred? Are there perspectives that are contradictory or seemingly confusing? Only by rightly divining the Word of truth can the eyes of our understanding be opened to God's perspective and not our own.

## Hate: A Scriptural Word Study

It is important that this investigation begin by examining the word *hate*, along with its various forms as it is used in both the Old and New Testaments. An examination of hate in its proper text and context will eliminate false assumptions, confusing interpretations, and erroneous perspectives.

Here are just a few examples of passages that could be misunderstood if not carefully examined. In Ecclesiastes 3:8, Solomon states, "There is a time to love and a time to hate." What is the author saying? Is he suggesting that there is a proper and specific time to love and to hate someone, some thing, or some event? Are people not to love others all the time?

Notice also the very words of Jesus Christ: "If any man comes to me, and hate not his father, and mother, and wife, and children, and brother, and sister, yea, and his own life also, he cannot be my disciple" (Luke 14:26). How should such a passage be understood when compared to "Honor thy father and thy mother" (Exodus 20:12), and "Husbands, love your wives" (Ephesians 5:25)? Why hate those closest to us?

Further, consider the paradoxical statement found in both Malachi 1:1–3 and Romans 9:13. God declared, "Jacob I have loved, but Esau I have hated." When taken at face value, this statement seems rather contradictory, coming from the lips of a God who describes Himself as a God of love. Understanding the word *hate* in its various forms and meanings will do much to clear up seemingly questionable passages.

In the Old Testament, the most commonly used Hebrew word for hate is the verb *sane*. It is used over 145 times and is used to connote jealousy, which is an "intense emotional reaction," or in a less emotional sense to mean "set against." It is used of persons, ideas, words, and inanimate objects. Genesis 37:4 is an example of the use of *sane* as it relates to jealousy. Because of their father, Jacob's, preference for Joseph, Joseph's brothers hated him; in other words, they were jealous of him. "And when his brethren saw that their father loved him more than all his brethren, they hated him, and could not speak peaceably unto him." In Genesis 37:18ff, *sane* is used in the sense of an outright hatred. Here, Joseph's brothers' deep-seated hatred caused them to act foolishly. At first, they decided to kill him, but in the end, they sold Joseph into slavery.

A milder use of the word *sane* is found in Exodus 18. It means "to be set against." "But select capable men from all the people—men who fear God, trustworthy men who hate dishonest gain and appoint them as officials over thousands, hundreds, fifties and tens" (v. 21). This advice was given to Moses by Jethro, his father-in-law. He encourages Moses to appoint men of integrity who were "set against" wrongdoing. The appointees were to assist Moses in the orderly and truthful judging of God's people.

In addition, *sane* is used to mean "to be unloved," "untrustworthy," and "unloved." Furthermore, in the sense of preference, *sane* can mean preferring someone or something over another, as in the case of Jacob's preferring Rachel over

*Dr. Clarence Talley Sr.*

Leah in Genesis 29:31: "And when the Lord saw that Leah was hated, he opened her womb: but Rachel was barren" (Vine 1984, 171).

Of all the Old Testament writers, it is the psalmist who most frequently used the Hebrew *sane*. Some form of the word occurs forty times in the book of Psalms. The psalmist spoke of his personal hatred for evil: "You who love the Lord hate evil! He protects the lives of his godly people and rescues them from the power of the wicked" (Psalm 97:10 NLT). He spoke of his hatred for deceit: "Each of your commandments is right. That is why I hate every false way" (Psalm 119:128). He spoke of his hatred for lying: "I hate and abhor all falsehood, but I love your instructions" (Psalm 119:163). Finally, the psalmist spoke of God's deliverance and destruction of his enemies who hated him: "He rescued me from my powerful enemies, from those who hated me and were too strong for me," and "You placed my foot on their necks. I have destroyed all who hated me" (Psalm 18:17, 40).

The primary New Testament Greek word for hate is the verb *miseo*. It is used in three contexts: (1) malicious and unjustifiable feelings, (2) of a right feeling and aversion from what is evil, and (3) relative preference for one thing over another (Vine 1984, 528).

In Matthew 10:22, Jesus said to His disciples, "And ye shall be hated of all men for my name's sake: but he that endureth to the end shall be saved." The use of the word here is in the sense of malicious and unjustifiable feelings toward the people of God by those who hate God.

The second use of the term *miseo*, to hate, is found in Revelation 2:6, where the people of God are to hate what God hates: "But this thou hast, that thou hatest the deeds of the Nicolaitanes, which I also hate." It is the proper attitude of holy opposition to all that is unholy. Accordingly, Hebrews 1:9 illustrates this same usage. It reads, "Thou hast loved righteousness, and hated iniquity; therefore God, even thy God, hath anointed thee with the oil of gladness above thy fellows."

Paul's observation of his own spiritual warfare shows how he hated sin, even in his own life: "I do not understand what I do. For what I want to do I do not do, but what I hate I do" (Romans 7:15 NIV).

The third use of the term *miseo* is related to a lesser degree of love. For example, Luke 14:26 states, "If any man come to me, and hate not his father, and mother, and wife, and children, and brethren, and sisters, yea, and his own life also, he cannot be my disciple." To hate one's relatives for the sake of Christ simply means to love them less than you love Christ and the things pertaining to the kingdom. It is an idiom of preference, meaning that one must prefer God above all else.

Matthew 10:37 expresses it this way: "He that loveth mother and father more than me, is not worthy of me: and he that loveth son or daughter more than me is not worthy of me." Moreover, in John 12:25 we read, "He that loveth his life shall lose it; and he that hateth his life in this world shall keep it unto life eternal." Hate, as used here, indicates a lesser value being placed on the believer's life in comparison to the claim of Christ. *When we value the things of God, we place less value on self, others, and the things of the world.* God has first place.

The Bible speaks with great clarity about a God of love who hates sin. His abhorrence for such is peppered throughout the pages of the Old and New Testaments. However, *divine hatred is opposition to sin, and it is not rooted in the natural.* Hate as an intense hostility and aversion is warned against in the Bible. It is synonymous with wickedness, and its origin is of the devil. Hate of a malicious nature is always condemned. The apostle John, writing to the early church that their joy may be full (1 John 1:4), warned them about their conduct toward one another. He said, "Whosoever hateth his brother is a murderer: and ye know that no murderer hath eternal life abiding in him" (1 John 3:15).

Christians are to love their enemies: "You have heard the law that says, 'Love your neighbor and hate your enemy. But I [Jesus] say, love your enemies! Pray for those who persecute you" (Matthew 5:43–44 NLT). On the other hand, hate their sins. We are to walk in love. We are to walk as children of the light. We are to have no fellowship with "the unfruitful works of darkness" (Ephesians 5:3–11).

In the succeeding chapters, we will examine seven things God hates that are revealed in Proverbs 6:16–19, beginning with "a proud look" and followed by "a lying tongue, And hands that shed innocent blood, A heart that deviseth wicked imaginations, Feet that be swift in running to mischief, A false witness that speaketh lies, And he that soweth discord among brethren."

We will look at these seven in detail. And although only seven are mentioned in this passage, the list is not exhaustive in the sense of its being finished. Seven is a round number and has biblical significance, but it is in no way absolute. Many other sins and temptations to which we give in are not listed in this passage but often are set before us by the tempter. All infringements found in God's Word are hateful in His sight. As a result, what is hateful to God must be hateful to believers. Just the knowledge of such should draw believers nearer to God, and we can never, ever allow these seven sins—or any others—to separate us from the love of God.

> What is hateful to God must be hateful to believers.

## Chapter 1 Study Questions

1. What is your definition of hate?

2. Define hate using a biblical dictionary.

3. In Luke 14:26, what did Jesus mean by asserting that hating was a prerequisite for discipleship?

4. What is the most commonly used word for *hate* in the Old Testament?

5. What are various meanings and usages for the Old Testament word *sane*?

6. What is the most commonly used word for *hate* in the New Testament?

*Dr. Clarence Talley Sr.*

7.  List the three contexts in which *miseo* is used in the New Testament.

8.  Divine hatred is opposition to sin, and it is not rooted in the _____.

9.  What is _____ to God must be _____ to believers.

# 2

# A PROUD LOOK

Although God is a God of love, He also expresses a hatred for that which is unholy, which means its adverse to His character. His disdain for and aversion to sin leaves Him no room to compromise with evil, as do men. God is the same "yesterday, today and forever" (Hebrews 13:8). Times have changed, but God has not. Times have changed, but sin has not. Sin yesterday is still sin today. No matter how society accepts or justifies ungodly behavior, God *still* hates sin. The redefining of sinful activities and lifestyles does not elevate ungodly behavior to a virtuous level. The sameness of God does not allow for such flip-flopping.

> The redefining of sinful activities and lifestyles does not elevate ungodly behavior to a virtuous level.

The message of ancient prophets against sin was "God hates it." The prophets proclaimed messages that addressed the conduct of God's people in light of what He required of them. The priests led in the worship of God, which pointed to His holiness. The king ruled the people of God according to God's dictates, but it was the prophet who declared, "Thus saith the Lord." Whenever the people of God did not live up to the His

*Dr. Clarence Talley Sr.*

expectations, God's prophets were always there to remind them of His displeasure.

Listen to the cry of the prophets on behalf of God: "I hate, I despise your religious festivals; your assemblies are a stench to me" (Amos 5:21 NIV). "'Do not plot evil against each other, and do not love to swear falsely. I hate all this,' declares the Lord" (Zechariah 8:17 NIV). "Because of all their wickedness in Gilgal, I hated them there. ... I will no longer love them; all their leaders are rebellious" (Hosea 9:15 NIV). Finally, in Malachi, the prophet expresses God's disdain for divorce: "'I hate divorce,' says the Lord, the God of Israel, 'because the man who divorces his wife covers his garment with violence'" (Malachi 2:16 NIV).

The enumeration of seven things God hates is found in Proverbs, as highlighted by the wise King Solomon, and we begin our exploration of each one here. Solomon wrote, "These six things doth the Lord hate: Yea, seven are an abomination unto him: A proud look, a lying tongue, And hands that shed innocent blood, A heart that deviseth wicked imaginations, Feet that be swift in running to mischief, A false witness that speaketh lies, And he that soweth discord among brethren" (Proverbs 6:16–19).

Obvious to this list are the terms for parts of the body— eyes, tongues, hands, heart, and feet. In and of themselves, these body parts are not evil, nor are they hated by the Lord. It is when they are used contrary to divine will that God abhors them. Our bodily organs must be used to glorify God and to bless others. Our eternal salvation is at stake. Notice the importance Jesus Christ put on the proper use of our appendages: "If your hand or your foot causes you to stumble, cut it off and throw it away. It is better for you to enter

> What is of eternal importance is eternal salvation, and we must accomplish it with fear and trembling.

life maimed or crippled than to have two hands or two feet and be thrown into eternal fire" (Matthew 18:8 NIV). Again, what is of eternal importance is eternal salvation, and we must accomplish it with fear and trembling.

The first thing God hates is a proud look, which means that God hates *pride*. Pride is the state or quality of being proud or having inordinate self-esteem; conceit concerning one's talents, ability, wealth, station, and more; disdainful behavior. These elements comprise the negative aspects of pride, but there also are positive aspects of the term as well.

The apostle Paul expressed a kind of positive pride: "I have spoken to you with great frankness; I take great pride in you. I am greatly encouraged; in all our troubles my joy knows no bounds" (2 Corinthians 7:4). Paul again expressed pride because of God's sufficient grace and what it had done for him. Paul argued, "Therefore I will boast all the more gladly about my weaknesses, so that Christ's power may rest on me" (2 Corinthians 12:9 NIV). As we can see, there is nothing wrong with a healthy degree of pride regarding an individual's person, position, or appearance. These are positive testimonies for Jesus Christ to the world (Harrison 1992). However, it is not this positive aspect of pride to which Solomon referred in his list.

Pride is first and foremost in our discussion "because it is at the bottom of all disobedience and rebellion against God's laws" (Spence and Exell 1974, 131). Pride is viewed as the root and essence of sin, and it has its origin in Satan. In Isaiah 14:13–15, he is identified as desiring to rise up and overthrow the kingdom of the one true God, saying, "*I will* ascend to heaven, *I will* raise my throne

> Satan is the architect of the inordinate "I, me, and mine mentality."

above the stars of God; *I will* sit enthroned on the mount of the assembly, on the utmost heights of the sacred mountain, *I will*

*Dr. Clarence Talley Sr.*

ascend above the tops of the clouds; *I will* make myself like the Most High" (italics mine). Thus, Satan sought for himself honor and glory that belong to God alone (Ezekiel 28). Satan is the architect of the inordinate "I, me, and mine mentality"—a negative mentality awash in selfishness. Since the fall in the garden of Eden, Satan has gone about deceiving man into having an attitude of pride and contempt toward God.

The majority of words for pride used in both the Old and New Testaments are overwhelmingly negative, and a "proud look" is no exception. It literally means *haughty or lofty eyes.* The word *proud* means *to be high,* which indicates a high and exalted attitude or arrogant behavior. It is a sin of attitude and of the heart and spirit.

Pride—arrogance—is named among the many sins practiced by evil men whom God has given over to a depraved mind. Their predicaments and sins are seen in Romans 1:28–31, which includes *pride*; these also are cited in 2 Timothy 3:1–4. Both passages reveal a list of evils men boldly will commit and flaunt in the last days. Note the list from Romans: "Unrighteousness, sexual immorality, wickedness, covetousness, maliciousness; full of envy, murder, strife, deceit, evil-mindedness; *they are* whisperers, backbiters, haters of God, violent, proud, boasters, inventors of evil things, disobedient to parents, undiscerning, untrustworthy, unloving, unforgiving, and unmerciful."

In addition to the enumeration of these evils, the Bible provides vivid pictures of a number of individuals who succumb to pride, and in many instances, it costs them dearly.

Pride compelled Pharaoh of Egypt to say to Moses, God's representative, "Who is the Lord, that I should obey his voice to let Israel go? I know not the Lord, neither will I let Israel go" (Exodus 5:2). In his arrogance, the pharaoh refused to let God's people go, and with each refusal, Pharaoh's heart slowly hardened toward God. Even after exceedingly great displays of God's power exhibited through Moses, his staff, and the plagues, the pharaoh still was indignant.

Subsequently, it was down at the Red Sea that God brought

*Seven Things God Hates*

the prideful pharaoh to his knees with the opening and closing of the Red Sea and the drowning of his elite army. The scene is vividly brought to life in Cecil B. DeMille's 1956 film *The Ten Commandments*, when the pharaoh, played by Yul Brynner, returns to his palace and the arms of his queen and at last admits, "Moses's God is God."

Another scriptural example is King Uzziah. Irrespective of his ingenuity and skilled leadership, King Uzziah's downfall was his pride. After becoming a popular and strong king and being characterized as one who "did what was right in the eyes of the Lord," Uzziah succumbed to pride (2 Kings 15:3; 2 Chronicles 26:4). He took it upon himself to do the work of the priests by offering incense before the Lord. He was unfaithful to the Lord his God and entered the temple of the Lord to burn incense on the altar of incense. Azariah, the priest, with eighty other courageous priests of the Lord, followed him in. They confronted King Uzziah and said, "It is not right for you, Uzziah, to burn incense to the Lord. That is for the priests, the descendants of Aaron, who have been consecrated to burn incense. Leave the sanctuary, for you have been unfaithful; and you will not be honored by the Lord God." Uzziah, who had a censer in his hand, ready to burn incense, became angry. While he was raging at the priests before the incense altar in the Lord's temple, leprosy broke out on his forehead (2 Chronicles 26:16–19 NIV). As a result, King Uzziah remained in this pitiful condition until the day he died.

Pride also caused King Nebuchadnezzar to credit himself with the rise and majesty of Babylon. He boldly observed, "Is not this the great Babylon I have built as the royal residence, by my mighty power and for the glory of my majesty?" (Daniel 4:30). As a result of his boasting, King Nebuchadnezzar suffered the loss

> "Pride goes before destruction and a haughty spirit before a fall."

of his faculties, and for seven years he was made to eat grass like cattle until the Lord restored his faculties. Daniel paints a vivid picture of the price of pride in the life of the king. For seven years, King Nebuchadnezzar was brought low because of his prideful spirit (Daniel 4:28–32). No wonder we are warned, "Pride goes before destruction and a haughty spirit before a fall" (Proverbs 16:18).

Luke 18:9–14 depicts an incident of religious pride in the form of arrogance and contemptible treatment of another individual. It is a parable told by Jesus of a Pharisee who, being lifted up in pride, trusted in himself while despising his fellow man. As the Pharisee prayed and compared himself to the tax collector, he gave a litany of reasons why he thought so highly of himself. No doubt the Pharisee expected his assessment of himself to be accepted by God as well. The Pharisee said, "God, I thank thee that I am not as other men are, extortioners, unjust, adulterers, or even as this publican" (Luke 18:11). The Pharisee even bragged about fasting and tithing (v. 12). Contrariwise to the Pharisee, the tax collector humbled himself before God and beseeched His mercy, simply praying, "God be merciful to me, a sinner" (v. 13).

Jesus declared that it was the tax collector who departed the temple "justified before God." The Pharisee, on the other hand, departed in the same condition in which he arrived—contemptible and proud and with the wrong estimation of himself. The words of Jesus are a warning to all: "For everyone who exalts himself will be humbled, and he who humbles himself will be exalted" (Luke 18:14). Solomon wisely conveyed something similar: "Pride brings a person low, but the lowly in spirit gain honor" (Proverbs 29:23 NIV).

> Pride promotes a false self-image and hinders spiritual growth.

The previous examples show us that a proud look fosters an evil and perverse way. Pride convinces

*Seven Things God Hates*

a person to trust in self and not God. Pride promotes a false self-image and hinders spiritual growth. Solomon warned, "Do you see a wise man in his own eyes? There is more hope for a fool than for him" (Proverbs 26:12 NIV). Solomon reasoned that a fool has more hope than a person filled with pride.

The apostle Paul cautioned the Christians in Rome, "Do not think of yourself more highly than you ought" (Romans 12:3). When we think more highly of ourselves than we should, we play the fool. Humility must be the aim of the believer.

> When we think more highly of ourselves than we should, we play the fool.

Pride will cause a person to believe that he or she can lie and never get caught, as in the case of Ananias and Sapphira. This husband and wife jointly sold a parcel of land. All the profits rightfully belonged to them, but in sharing with the Christian community of the early church, they lied to the Holy Spirit about the proceeds earned. As a result, they fell dead before God (Acts 5:1–11).

Similarly, Joshua 7 provides an example of pride bolstering the belief that one can steal and never be found out. The culprit, Achan, however, found out the hard way and paid with his life and the lives of his loved ones.

In 2 Kings 5:20–27, Gehazi, the servant of the prophet Elisha, allowed his national pride to cloud his judgment when he coveted the gold and the silver of the Syrian general Naaman. Gehazi's covetousness caused him to deceive Naaman and to lie to Elisha. Like the unfortunate King Uzziah, Gehazi contracted a lifelong case of leprosy. Pride's companion is always deception.

When the popular King Hezekiah was delivered from the hands of death, he failed to be thankful for God's mercy and became caught up in pride. As a result, Hezekiah's pride brought God's anger against the king, Judah, and Jerusalem. Yet when

"Hezekiah repented of the pride of his heart, as did the people of Jerusalem ... the Lord's wrath did not come on them during the days of Hezekiah" (2 Kings 20:13; 2 Chronicles 32:25–26).

No individual or group of individuals is exempt from the destructive forces of pride. God warned Israel of the eminent threat of pride upon their entry into the Promised Land. Through Moses, God cautioned, "Beware that you do not forget the Lord your God by not keeping His commandments and His ordinances and His statutes which I am commanding you today; otherwise, when you have eaten and are satisfied, and have built good houses and lived *in them*, and when your herds and your flocks multiply, and your silver and gold multiply, and all that you have multiplies, then your heart will become proud and you will forget the Lord your God" (Deuteronomy 8:11–14a NASB). Holy remembrance for what God had done was to be the cure for Israel's future lapse in memory, brought on by pride.

> History's highway is strewn with nations that have fallen as a direct or indirect result of pride and its influences.

History's highway is strewn with nations that have fallen as a direct or indirect result of pride and its influences. Israel and Judah and many of the nations surrounding them fell prey to pride and ultimately met God's judgment.

Consider further, for example, the pride of the nation of Edom, descendants of Esau, who, like the eagle, had built their habitation high in the mountains and felt that no one could defeat them. But God said, "The pride of your heart has deceived you, you who live in the clefts of the rocks and make your home on the

> Pride demotes God and lifts up self.

*Seven Things God Hates*

heights, you who say to yourself, 'Who can bring me down to the ground?' Though you soar like the eagle and make your nest among the stars, from there I will bring you down" (Obadiah 3–4). The pride of the Edomites prompted them to believe they were untouchable and invincible. God saw differently, and He responded by sending judgment.

In concluding our discussion of a proud look, it again must be asserted that God hates pride. It is the root of sin. Its origin is the devil. It perpetuates a false self-image. It causes one to despise others. Pride destroys individuals and brings down nations. Pride demotes God and lifts up self. The end results of pride are corruption, shame, and destruction. The Lord guarantees it (Isaiah 14:22).

Let me remind you once again of scripture's admonishment: "Pride goes before destruction and a haughty spirit before a fall" (Proverbs 16:18). On the other hand, humility is what the Lord requires of His people. James 4:10 makes a promise to believers: "Humble yourselves in the sight of the Lord, and he shall lift you up." James and Peter also exclaimed to believers, "Clothe yourselves with humility towards one another" because "God opposes the proud but gives grace to the humble" (James 4:6; 1 Peter 5:5).

Moreover, God assures the humble, "These are the ones I look on with favor: those who are humble and contrite in spirit" (Isaiah 66:2b NIV). But to the proud, God promises to "Unleash the fury of [His] wrath, to look at every proud man and bring him low, look at every proud man and humble him, crush the wicked where they stand" (Job 40:11–12 NIV). God hates pride.

## Chapter 2 Study Questions

1. When it comes to evil, why is God unable to flip-flop or vacillate like man?

2. List the organs that are mentioned in Proverbs 6:16–19.

3. Define pride.

4. The positive aspects of pride are a testimony for _____ to the world.

5. _____ is the root of sin, and it has its origin in _____.

6. Pride is a sin of_____ and of the _____ and _____.

*Seven Things God Hates*

7. Pride caused the pharaoh of Egypt to refuse to let

_____

_____

8. Pride caused King Uzziah to enter the temple of the Lord to burn _____.

9. Pride caused King Nebuchadnezzar to credit himself with the rise and majesty of _____.

10. Pride promotes a false _____ and hinders spiritual _____.

11. A close companion of pride is always _____. Give two biblical examples.

12. Pride _____ God and lifts up _____.

*Dr. Clarence Talley Sr.*

13. What is the antidote to pride?




14. What has God promised to do to every proud man?

# 3

# A LYING TONGUE

The second item from Solomon's list of seven things God hates is a lying tongue. To lie is to speak falsely. It is any statement or act that is meant to deceive—verbal and nonverbal acts that portray something known to be false (Harrison 1992, 242). Stated another way, "Lying is the willful perversion of truth, not only by speech, but by any means whatever whereby a false impression is conveyed to the mind" (Spence and Exell 1974, 131). Therefore, a lie can take many forms—a hypocritical lifestyle (Jeremiah 23:14; Matthew 23:1–33; 1 Timothy 4:2), a false system (Romans 3:7), error (1 John 2:21), and the denial of Jesus Christ (1 John 2:22) all reveal falsehood.

*Sheqer* is the most frequently used Old Testament word for a lie. Sheqer defines a way of life that is contrary to the law of God. It denotes deceptive speech: "Your lips have spoken lies, and your tongue hath muttered perverseness" (Isaiah 59:3), and "Then the Lord said unto me, 'The prophets prophesy lies in my name. I have not sent them or appointed them or spoken to them'" (Jeremiah 14:14). Sheqer may also denote deceptive character, as in Jeremiah 23:14: "I have seen also in the prophets of Jerusalem a horrible thing: they commit adultery, and walk in lies" (Vine 1984, 125).

In the New Testament, *pseudos* is a commonly used noun that means falsehood or lie. It is used in John 8:44 in reference to Satan. Jesus spoke these words about him: "When he lies,

*Dr. Clarence Talley Sr.*

he speaks his native language, for he is a liar and the father of lies." In Romans 1:25, the apostle Paul spoke of the depraved condition of man, asserting, "[Mankind] exchanged the truth of God for a lie." And in 2 Thessalonians 2:11, a delusion sent by God caused those who did not accept Him to believe a lie (Vine 1984, 664).

Also in the New Testament, the verb form is *pseudo*, which means to deceive by lies. It is used in such passages as the following:

"Blessed are you when people insult you, persecute you and falsely say all kinds of evil against you because of me" (Matthew 5:11). "I speak the truth in Christ—I am not lying, my conscience confirms it through the Holy Spirit" (Romans 9:1). "The God and Father of the Lord Jesus, who is to be praised forever, knows that I am not lying" (2 Corinthians 11:31). And finally, "Do not lie to each other, since you have taken off your old self with its practices" (Colossians 3:9).

The old self encourages deception by wearing a lie. The new self no longer wears that old garment of deception by lies.

> The new self no longer wears that old garment of deception by lies.

Another frequently used word associated with lying, falsehood, and deception is *hupokrisis*. Its primary meaning was "to answer." Later, it became used of actors— those who pretend. Finally, it came to mean hypocrisy. It is used in Matthew 23:28, "But within ye are full of hypocrisy and iniquity," and in Mark 12:15, "But he knowing their hypocrisy, said unto them, Why tempt ye me?" The noun form of the word is *hypocrite*, and it too is used a number of times to denote deceptive acts.

Jesus exposed the true character of the Pharisees and the deception in their hearts when He said, "Isaiah was right when he prophesied about you hypocrites; as it is written: 'These people honor me with their lips, but their hearts are far from me'" (Mark 7:6). Again, Jesus warned the Pharisees, "You hypocrite, first take the plank out of your eye, and then you will see clearly to remove the speck from your brother's eye" (Luke 6:42). Christ used the term *hypocrite* fifteen times in Matthew. He was particularly upset by the duplicity among religious leaders who acted out lies among the people. Matthew 23 is especially awash in Jesus's condemnation of the Pharisees and the scribes, for their hypocrisy hurt themselves and God's people, whom they were charged to lead in righteousness.

With woe after woe, Jesus condemned the religious leaders of His day because they stifled religious freedom, pretended to be holy, converted others to deceive, made vows to circumvent duty, omitted the important to do the unimportant, looked clean but were diseased, and, last, possessed a phony holiness and evil intent that exceeded their forefathers (Matthew 23:13–30). Our Lord's "woes" to those who played to public applause shows His disdain for those who speak and/or perform a lie (Vine 1984, 571).

> Man may practice the dark art of lying, but it is impossible for God to lie.

Falsehood, craftiness, hypocrisy, deception, and error are all akin to a lying tongue and contrary to godliness. Consequently, God hates a lying tongue because it is contrary to His nature. He is "merciful and gracious, longsuffering, and abounding in goodness and truth" (Exodus 34:6). The Lord is a "God of truth and without iniquity, just and right is he" (Deuteronomy 32:4). Man may practice the dark art of lying, but it is impossible for God to lie (Titus 1:2; Hebrews 6:18). "God is not a man that he should lie" (Numbers 23:19).

> God is truth; to argue anything less would be a lie.

*Dr. Clarence Talley Sr.*

To His disciples, Jesus Christ, the Son of God, revealed Himself as the embodiment of truth. He said, "I am the way, the truth, and the life." John the Baptist described Him as the word made flesh, full of grace and truth (John 1:14, 17). Upon His departure from the earthly scene, Christ promised to send His followers "the Spirit of truth," the Comforter, the Holy Spirit (John 14:17; 15:26). God is truth; to argue anything less would be a lie, and He detests liars.

Like pride, the origin of lies and lying resides in the bosom of Satan. He is the enemy of the truth and is aptly described as the father of lies. In speaking to the Pharisees, who sought to kill Jesus because of the truth He spoke, Jesus attributed the source of their desires to Satan. Jesus said, "Ye are of your father the devil, and the lusts of your father ye will do. He was a murderer from the beginning, and abode not in the truth, because there is no truth in him. When he speaketh a lie, he speaketh of his own: for he is a liar, and the father of it. And because I tell you the truth, ye believe me not" (John 8:43–44).

> Sowing evil is not just what Satan does; it's who he is—the sower of evil.

As the originator of all that is evil, Satan was thrown out of the sphere of truth—heaven—only to make his abode in the pavilion of falsehood. In the garden of Eden, he deceived Eve into believing the first lie: "You shall not surely die" (Genesis 3:4). In 1 Timothy, we are told, "And Adam was not the one deceived; it was the women who was deceived and became a sinner" (vv. 13–14). Wrapped up in the first lie were

> Truth to Satan is anything but the Word of God.

evil seeds of "the lust of the flesh, the lust of the eyes, and the pride of life" (1 John 2:16).

These seeds are the sole property of Satan. Lying is the nature of the devil. He is wholly opposed to truth. Truth to Satan is anything but the Word of God, and because of his irrevocable stance, he and all his followers are an abomination to God (Proverbs 12:22; Psalm 119:163). Satan is always prepared to plant tares of lies in the garden of the believer's heart. Sowing evil is not just what Satan does; it's who he is—the sower of evil. His actions can be seen in a parable Jesus spoke. The parable details the sabotaging actions of the sower of evil:

> The kingdom of heaven is like a man who sowed good seed in his field. But while everyone was sleeping, his enemy came and sowed weeds among the wheat, and went away. When the wheat sprouted and formed heads, then the weeds also appeared.
>
> The owner's servants came to him and said, "Sir, didn't you sow good seed in your field? Where then did the weeds come from?"
>
> "An enemy did this," he replied.
>
> "The servants asked him, "Do you want us to go and pull them up?"
>
> "No," he answered, "because while you are pulling the weeds, you may uproot the wheat with them. Let both grow together until the harvest. At that time I will tell the harvesters: First collect the weeds and tie them in bundles to be burned; then gather the wheat and bring it into my barn." (Matthew 13:24–30 NIV)

*Dr. Clarence Talley Sr.*

Whether for deceit, lies, or shrewd manipulation, the sower of evil is, in the end, judged by Jesus Christ, a point clearly made in the parable. The Bible could not be any clearer on God's abhorrence of a lying tongue. It strictly forbids and warns against it. Whether your opinion is that it is an insignificant rearranging of the facts, a so-called little white lie, a known omission of vital information that significantly alters truth, or an action that is meant to deceive, it is still a lie. The shrewd manipulation of words with the intent to deceive is always the work of Satan.

> The shrewd manipulation of words with the intent to deceive is always the work of Satan.

In describing the destructive power of the sins of the tongue, it has been said, "Loose lips sink ships." Loose lips will destroy marriages. Loose lips will divide churches. Loose lips will break up friendships. Loose lips will plant you in the unemployment line, and loose lips can get you killed. Loose lips and wagging tongues are both dangerous and destructive.

Accordingly, James describes the tongue as "a restless evil, full of deadly poison" that we must guard against (James 3:8). Loose, poisonous lips will bring about corruption and destruction. They will sink both saint and sinner. As a result, the Bible warns, "Do not lie. Do not deceive one another" (Leviticus 19:11). "Do not lie to each other, since you have taken off your old self with its practices" (Colossians 3:9). "A truthful witness does not deceive, but a false witness pours out lies" (Proverbs 14:5). "Therefore each of you must put off falsehood and speak truthfully to his neighbor, for we are all members of one body" (Ephesians 4:25 NIV).

The classic story of Ananias and Sapphira in Acts 5:1–10 illustrates the enormous consequences that God ordains for the sin of lying. The passage is as follows:

*Seven Things God Hates*

But a certain man named Ananias, with Sapphira his wife, sold a possession, And kept back part of the price, his wife also being privy to it, and brought a certain part, and laid it at the apostles' feet. But Peter said, "Ananias, why hath Satan filled thine heart to lie to the Holy Ghost, and to keep back part of the price of the land? Whiles it remained, was it not thine own? And after it was sold, was it not in thine own power? Why hast thou conceived this thing in thine heart? Thou hast not lied unto men, but unto God." And Ananias hearing these words fell down, and gave up the ghost: and great fear came on all them that heard these things. And the young men arose, wound him up, and carried him out, and buried him. And it was about the space of three hours after, when his wife, not knowing what was done, came in. And Peter answered unto her, "Tell me whether ye sold the land for so much?" And she said, "Yea, for so much." Then Peter said unto her, "How is it that ye have agreed together to tempt the Spirit of the Lord? Behold, the feet of them which have buried thy husband are at the door, and shall carry thee out." Then fell she down straightway at his feet, and yielded up the ghost: and the young men came in, and found her dead, and, carrying her forth, buried her by her husband.

Ananias and Sapphira were husband and wife who acted out a lie. They were a deceptive tag team. They sold a piece of property and surreptitiously kept back part of the profit. When they presented their offering to the church, however, they presented it as the total profit of the sale. The apostle Peter, the leader of the early church, discerned their deception and

*Dr. Clarence Talley Sr.*

rebuked them. Peter warned that they had "not lied to men but to God." As a result, they both fell dead on the spot.

The lies Ananias and Sapphira told and their dramatic end are known to many. But they are not the only biblical characters who found it expedient to lie for some reason or another. Cain lied to God after killing his brother and being questioned by God. "Then the Lord said to Cain, 'Where is your brother Abel?' 'I don't know,' he replied. 'Am I my brother's keeper?'" (Genesis 4:9).

Abraham lied to the Egyptian pharaoh by pretending Sarah, his wife, was his sister (Genesis 12:11–19). On another occasion, Sarah, after eavesdropping and laughing about her prophesied pregnancy, lied to the angel, who was aware of her emotional outburst and who had predicted her future condition. Secretly, Sarah did laugh. Secretly, Sarah did ask, "Will I really have a child, now that I am old?" Sarah's lie, coupled with her doubt, led the angel to ask, "Is anything too hard for the Lord" (Genesis 18:1–15).

Isaac, the promised son of Abraham, also lied about Rebekah, his wife, pretending she too was his sister (Genesis 26:7–10). Jacob, son of Isaac, lied to his father about his identity to steal his brother Esau's birthright (Genesis 27). The jealous sons of Jacob lied to their father about the death of his favorite son, Joseph, when in actuality they had sold him into slavery (Genesis 37:31–36).

Potiphar's wife, caught up in her lust, lied to Potiphar about their house servant Joseph when she accused him of attempted rape (Genesis 39:4–17).

Gehazi lied to Naaman about the needs of his master, Elisha, in order to deceive him out of his silver and gold. Upon returning to his master's house, Gehazi lied again; he lied to Elisha about his whereabouts (2 Kings 5:21–27). Gehazi paid dearly for his deceit; he contracted leprosy.

Laban lied to Jacob. He tricked him into marrying his firstborn daughter, Leah, although Laban had agreed to give Jacob his second-born daughter, Rachel (Genesis 29:15–30).

*Seven Things God Hates*

Saul lied to Samuel about the destruction of the Amalekites (1 Samuel 15:13). Herod lied to the wise men about wanting to worship the baby Jesus when his plan was to kill Him (Matthew 2:8).

And Peter lied to the damsel who identified him as a follower of Jesus. Three different times Peter exclaimed passionately, "I don't know the man" (Matthew 26:69–75).

Among this incomplete list, we also find ourselves, for we have all sinned and come short of the glory of God. Unlike Ananias and Sapphira's penalty, we may not fall dead in our tracks the moment we sin, but each sin acts to dissolve our intimate relationship with God. Sin always carries consequences with it.

The Word teaches that the wages of sin are high, and liars will not escape. A liar will face the severest kind of punishment. Scripture instructs that "a sword is upon the liar," and "a false witness will not go unpunished and he who pours out lies will not go free (Jeremiah 50:36; Proverbs 19:5).

> Sin always carries consequences with it.

In addition, the liar will be destroyed and his mouth silenced (Psalm 5:6; 63:11). Certainly, the liar may reap the pleasures of his sins for a season, but his joy is short-lived. His "lying tongue lasts only for a moment," and his "lying lips" will be "put to silence" (Proverbs 12:19; Psalm 31:18).

Furthermore, those who tell untruths will have their part in the lake of fire (Revelation 21:8). They will forever be barred from heaven. "Nothing impure will ever enter [heaven], nor will anyone who does what is shameful or deceitful" (Revelation 21:27). "He that worketh deceit shall not dwell within my house: he that telleth lies shall not tarry in my sight" (Psalm 101:7).

Revelation 22:15 confirms the exclusion of those from the New Jerusalem who have lived contrary to the will of the Father. "Outside are the dogs, those who practice magic arts, the

*Dr. Clarence Talley Sr.*

sexually immoral, the murderers, the idolaters, and everyone who loves and practice falsehood." These workers of iniquity will not enter the kingdom of heaven.

In summary, the God of truth hates a lying tongue. Whether the act of lying is verbal or nonverbal, it is condemned. It is the work of the devil, and everyone who does not speak the truth is doing the work of the devil. The simple warning of scripture is "do not lie." The consequences are grave and even deadly. Hence, the challenge to Christians is not to practice the dark art of lying. To meet this challenge, believers must seek to please the Father by following the example of Jesus Christ who said, "For I always do what pleases him" (John 8:29).

Therefore, we must believe and know the truth (1 Timothy 4:3). We must walk in the truth (3 John 3; 4). We must obey the truth (1 Peter 1:22). We must be established in the truth (2 Peter 1:12). And finally, we must speak the truth and wear the truth as a garment (Ephesians 4:15; 6:14). Believers do all these things because they know that "truthful lips endure forever," but the Lord hates a "lying tongue."

## Chapter 3 Study Questions

1. Define a lying tongue.

2. What forms can lying take?

3. What is the most frequently used word for lying in the Old Testament?

4. Define *sheqer*.

5. Sheqer may denote deception by _____ and/or _____.

6. What is the most frequently used word in the New Testament for lying or falsehood?

7. Who is the "father of lies"?

*Dr. Clarence Talley Sr.*

8. _____ is also associated with lying, falsehood, and deception.

9. During Jesus's earthly ministry, who acted out lies among the people?

10. What were some of the hypocritical acts of the Pharisees that offended Jesus?

11. Falsehood, craftiness, hypocrisy, and error are all akin to a _____ and contrary to _____.

12. Man may practice the dark art of lying, but it is _____ for God to lie.

13. Who is the enemy of truth?

14. The shrewd manipulation of words with the intent to deceive is always the work of _____.

*Seven Things God Hates*

15. What are the warnings found in Leviticus 19:11 and in Colossians 3:9?

16. Why do you think Ananias and Sapphira agreed to lie about the amount earned in the sale of their property?

17. List two biblical characters who chose to lie, and state the consequences that arose because of it.

18. According to Proverbs 12:19 and Psalm 31:18, a "lying tongue last only for a _____" and "lying lips" will be "put to _____."

19. Where is the final abode of a lying tongue?

# 4

# HANDS THAT SHED INNOCENT BLOOD

We live in a violent world—a world where the shedding of innocent blood has become all too commonplace. The innocent blood of unsuspecting individuals is spilled on our streets, in our homes, in the workplace, and even in our churches. The shocking cannibalistic homicides of Jeffrey Dahmer and others make us painfully aware of man's inhumanity to man.

> The shedding of innocent blood by those in authority and by those who have sought revenge by any means necessary has left the streets of our nation and the world stained with blood.

Another unthinkable event is the James Byrd incident in Jasper, Texas, where a black man was chained to the back of a pickup truck and dragged through the streets until dead. The murders carried out by Andrea Yates, a Texas mother of five who methodically drowned all five of her children, is another horrific incident. Etched in the minds of Americans is September 11, 2001—a day that stunned the world.

Recently, the notable tragic events such as the Columbine High School massacre, the Virginia Tech shooting, the Tucson shooting, the Sandy Hook Elementary

*Seven Things God Hates*

School shooting, the Charleston church shooting, the Orlando nightclub shooting, the Las Vegas shooting, and most recently, the Sutherland Spring Church tragedy have all reminded us of humankind's propensity for the destruction of innocent life. Sadly, the shedding of innocent blood by those in authority and by those who have sought revenge by any means necessary has left the streets of our nation and the world stained with blood.

In any given twenty-four-hour period, we cannot avoid being confronted with the third thing that God hates: "Hands that shed innocent blood." Life is sacred and precious to God, as the psalmist declared: "Precious in the sight of the Lord is the death of his faithful saint" (Psalm 116:15). Therefore, the sanctity of life should matter to humans, especially God-fearing men and women.

Life should not be taken for granted or needlessly snuffed out; all lives matter. Humans are the crown of creation, created in God's image and likeness, with a plan and purpose for their brief stay on earth (Jeremiah 29:11). The unlawful killing of one person by another, especially with premeditated malice, is an abomination in God's sight.

A late theologian compiled five reasons why taking a life maliciously is no trifling matter. He concluded that it (1) is a crime against God, (2) is a crime against society, (3) is a crime against the family unit, (4) is a crime against the individual whose life is cut short, and (5) reveals a hatred of God's image. "Hands that shed innocent blood," more familiarly referred to as murder, is a horrendous crime in the eyes of civilized society, the families it affects, and in the eyes of God.

Murder, much like pride and lying, has its genesis in Satan: "He was a murderer from the beginning" (John 8:44). The first crime recorded in the Bible is murder. We read about it in Genesis 4: "And Cain talked with Abel his brother: and it came to pass, when they were in the field, that Cain rose up against Abel his brother, and slew him" (v. 8). Cain murdered his brother in a fit of jealousy and plunged humanity into mayhem and violence. God expressed His displeasure with Cain's murderous act. "And

*Dr. Clarence Talley Sr.*

he said, 'What hast thou done? The voice of thy brother's blood crieth unto me from the ground'" (Genesis 4:10). Following these words, Cain's judgment, punishment, and banishment were announced by God.

He told Cain, "Now you are under a curse and driven from the ground, which opened its mouth to receive your brother's blood from your hand. When you work the ground, it will no longer yield its crops for you. You will be a restless wanderer on the earth." Cain said to the Lord, "My punishment is more than I can bear. Today you are driving me from the land, and I will be hidden from your presence; I will be a restless wanderer on the earth, and whoever finds me will kill me." But the Lord said to him, "Not so; anyone who kills Cain will suffer vengeance seven times over." Then the Lord put a mark on Cain so that no one who found him would kill him (Genesis 4:11–15 NIV).

In Genesis 4:8 and also verses 14–15, we have the first use of the word *harag*, which means to kill, slay, and destroy. It is used considerably throughout the Old Testament. *Harag* is not the same word used in the Mosaic Law, where we find the admonition against murder—"Thou shall not kill" (Exodus 20:13). The word used there is *ratsach,* a term that implies premeditated killing, thus better translating the commandment as "do not murder." Nevertheless, "Hands that shed innocent blood" are singled out in the Ten Commandments; thus, long before Proverbs 6, God's abhorrence of such an act was made quite clear (Vine 1984, 209).

> To commit murder is to exercise a blow against God and everything He represents.

Genesis 9:6 plainly states why murder is forbidden. It reads, "Whoever sheds the blood of man, by man shall his blood be shed; for in the image of God has God made man." Made in the image and likeness of God, man is closely akin to God. To commit murder is to exercise a blow against God and

*Seven Things God Hates*

everything He represents. And to such action, God says, "I hate it."

"Hands that shed innocent blood" is defined as *premeditative murder* as opposed to *unintentional killing*. The Old Testament thus recognizes the distinction and makes proper provisions. When someone killed unintentionally, the Law provided six cities of refuge where a person could flee and seek asylum. "Then the Lord said to Joshua: 'Tell the Israelites to designate the cities of refuge, as I instructed you through Moses, so that anyone who kills a person accidentally and unintentionally may flee there and find protection from the avenger of blood'" (Joshua 20:1–3; also see Numbers 35 and Deuteronomy 19).

If a person was found guilty of unintentional manslaughter, he was to stay in a designated city of refuge until the death of the high priest. If a person left the city before that time, he or she did so at his or her own peril (Numbers 35:26–28).

Those found guilty of *premeditated* murder received the appropriate punishment under the law. They were to be given a trial and witnesses were to testify (Exodus 35:30). If found guilty, they were put to death. "Anyone who strikes a person with a fatal blow is to be put to death" (Exodus 21:12; Numbers 35:16).

In the New Testament, Jesus Christ imposed a more spiritual dimension to the act of murder by closely associating murder with anger. Jesus taught that it was not just the physical act of taking another's life, important as that may be, but the condition of a man's heart that sets the stage for horrific acts such as murder. He said, "But the things that come out of the mouth come from the heart, and these make a man 'unclean.' For out of the heart come evil thoughts, murder, adultery, sexual immorality, theft, false testimony, slander" (Matthew 15:18–9). Murder, as interpreted by Jesus, is first a condition of the heart.

> Anger in the heart can lead to blood on the hands.

Consequently, anger in the heart, Jesus exclaimed, can lead to blood on the hands. Thus, anger must be guarded against. The apostle John added another dimension. He said, "Whosoever hateth his brother is a murderer" (1 John 3:15). James, writing to the twelve tribes (1:1), concluded that the cause of murder is rooted in the evil desires for pleasure that lurks within the individual. James exclaimed, "What causes fights and quarrels among you? Don't they come from your desires that battle within you?" (4:1) In addition, the apostle Paul listed murder as one of the corruptible works of the flesh (Galatians 5:21).

In the first murder, Cain killed his brother Abel in a jealous rage. Other biblical characters also have acted rashly. For example, Moses slew an Egyptian due to anger over the mistreatment of a Hebrew (Exodus 2:11–12). Herod killed all the little children in Bethlehem who were two years old and younger because of his insecurity and anger toward the wise men (Matthew 2:16). In Acts 7, Stephen was stoned to death because the Jews were upset over his effectual and fervent preaching and defense of the faith. In their rage and hard-heartedness, "they shook their fists at him in rage" (Acts 7:54) and "dragged him out of the city and began to stone him" (Acts 7:58). What is common to each of these incidents is the element of *anger*—anger in the heart.

Jesus further identifies murderers as those who harbor anger and speak contemptuously about their brother. Jesus said, "You have heard it said to the people long ago, 'Do not murder, and anyone who murders will be subject to the judgment.' But I tell you anyone who is angry with his brother will be subject to judgment. Again, anyone who says to his brother, 'Racca,' is answerable to the Sanhedrin. But anyone who says, 'You fool!' will be in danger of the fire of hell" (Matthew 5:21–22 NIV).

Jesus contends that *murder in the heart* is just as sinful as the actual deed. Just because a person fails to act out what he thinks and desires to do does not exonerate that individual. Many would argue that since they don't commit the act, they

*Seven Things God Hates*

are not guilty of shedding of innocent blood. Jesus's teaching about murder is opposed to this kind of exonerative reasoning. As a result, this places many of us in the guilty category.

Jesus explained, "You have heard that it was said, 'Do not commit adultery.' But I tell you that anyone who looks at a woman lustfully has already committed adultery with her in his heart" (Matthew 5:27–28). Jesus condemns the act of lust/consummation that occurs in the heart, even though the onlooker never outwardly acts on his or her inner desires. To give a rock to the thrower or to financially reward an assassin while hiding in the shadows does not negate one's involvement. To murder overtly or covertly, according to Jesus, is still murder. Your hands may not have committed the crime, but in your heart, you participated fully.

> Your hands may not have committed the crime, but in your heart, you participated fully.

We must remember that what we do, think, or feel does not escape God. Our inner thoughts are always an open book before Him. He knows us when we are asleep and awake, at work or play, and most of all, He knows our motivations and desires. When we masquerade, we may manage to hide the intent of the heart from our peers because their primary focus is on the outer man. However, "The Lord does not look at the things people looks at. People look

> With perfect knowledge, God is intimately and infinitely aware of the possible actions, scenarios, and choices of all men; nothing escapes Him.

*Dr. Clarence Talley Sr.*

at the outward appearance, but the Lord looks at the heart" (1 Samuel 16:7 NIV).

The suit, the tie, the Ralph Lauren brand, and the Gucci logo may all be seen by humankind, but inward corruption and hypocrisy is always seen by God. With perfect knowledge, God is intimately and infinitely aware of the possible actions, scenarios, and choices of all men; nothing escapes Him. Jesus said to the Pharisees, "On the outside you appear to people as righteous but on the inside you are full of hypocrisy and wickedness" (Matthew 23:28). God's assessment of us starts with our hearts. He measures from the inside out. "For as a man thinketh in his heart so is he" (Proverbs 23:7). God hates the individual who commits murder in his or her heart as much as He hates those who actually physically murder.

The chief priests and the Pharisees fit the former category.

They were guilty in the death of Jesus of Nazareth, just as if they had personally driven the nails in His hands and the spikes in His feet.

They hired Judas, the betrayer. "Then one of the Twelve— the one called Judas Iscariot—went to the chief priests and asked, 'What are you willing to give me if I deliver him over to you?' So they counted out for him thirty pieces of silver" (Matthew 26:14–15).

They held a mock trial at night with false witnesses. "The chief priests and the whole Sanhedrin were looking for false evidence against Jesus so that they could put him to death. But they did not find any, though many false witnesses came forward" (Matthew 26:59–60).

They took counsel to put him to death. "Early in the morning, all the chief priests and the elders of the people made their plans how to have Jesus executed" (Matthew 27:1).

They took Jesus to Pilate with false charges and envy (Matthew 27:2–25), and they encouraged the release of a guilty man over an innocent one. "But the chief priests and the elders persuaded the crowd to ask for Barabbas and to have Jesus executed. … 'What shall I do, then, with Jesus who is called

*Seven Things God Hates*

the Messiah?' Pilate asked. They all answered, 'Crucify him!' ... Then he released Barabbas to them. But he had Jesus flogged, and handed him over to be crucified" (Matthew 27:20, 22, 26).

Consequently, the chief priests and the Pharisees' hands may not have appeared dirty, but they were hands that shed innocent blood nonetheless.

For millennia now, the cries of innocent blood, like Abel's, have ascended to heaven, from the first murder in Eden to today's high-profile murders to murderous acts that have gone undiscovered or unsolved by the finest detectives. God is perfectly aware of the shedding of innocent blood and will exact justice at the appointed time. Isaiah warned, "See, the Lord is coming out of his dwelling to punish the people of the earth for their sins. The earth will disclose the blood shed on it; the earth will conceal its slain no longer" (Isaiah 26:21 NIV). Murderers, among others, will have their part in eternal flames (Revelation 21:8).

Perpetually, we must remember that man is made in the image and likeness of God. He is the crown of His creation and the apple of His eye. Into man's nostrils, God has blown the breath of life. To act feloniously against others is to come under the judgment of God. Whether we maliciously malign with the tongue, or kill with a weapon of choice, or harbor murder in our hearts, the Lord has sworn to punish and avenge the blood of the innocent.

Whether we act individually, corporately, nationally, or internationally, the shedding of innocent blood is hated by God.

> To act feloniously against others is to come under the judgment of God.

## Chapter 4 Study Questions

1. Man is the crown of creation, created in God's _____ and _____.

2. Murder has its genesis in _____.

3. The first crime recorded in the Bible is _____.

4. _____ committed the first murder.

5. What penalty did God impose on Cain?

6. Define *harag*.

7. What Hebrew word for murder is used in the sixth commandment of the Ten Commandments?

*Seven Things God Hates*

8. To commit murder is to exercise a blow against _____ and _____ He represents.

9. "Hands that shed innocent blood" is defined as _____ as opposed to _____.

10. What provisions were made for *unintentional killing?*

11. What was the penalty for those found guilty of *premeditated murder?*

12. Explain the spiritual dimension of murder as interpreted by Jesus Christ in the New Testament.

13. What was the apostle John's perspective on a murderer?

14. *Murder in the heart* is just as sinful as the _____.

*Dr. Clarence Talley Sr.*

15. Inward corruption and hypocrisy are always seen by
_____.

16. What will be the end of those who shed innocent blood?

# 5

# A HEART THAT DEVISES WICKED IMAGINATIONS

Naturally, man has a heart condition that is contrary to God. We would like to believe "I'm okay; you're okay," but that is not what the Bible teaches. Psychologists, sociologists, legislators, religious leaders, and self-help authors all have attempted to paint a positive picture of humankind. They have tried to convince us that man is not all that bad, but, again, that is not what the Bible teaches.

It may be cliché to say, "You don't know my heart," but truthfully speaking, no one really knows the heart of another person. When we turn to the Scripture, however, the condition of one's heart is an open book. The Bible is quite specific about the condition of the human heart. Jeremiah 17:9 says, "The heart is deceitful above all things, and desperately wicked: who can know it?"

The Lord's own analysis of the heart is "the imagination of man's heart is evil from his youth" (Genesis 8:21). Unless the spirit

> Unless the spirit of man is renewed, with God as the head of man's life, the desperately wicked nature of man will have its way—a way that is corrupt and destructive.

*Dr. Clarence Talley Sr.*

of man is renewed, with God as the head of man's life, the desperately wicked nature of man will have its way—a way that is corrupt and destructive.

With this in mind, we now turn our attention to a fourth thing that God hates: a heart that deviseth wicked imaginations. This abomination is best approached by examining three key words in the passage—*heart, deviseth,* and *imaginations.*

The first key word is *heart.* The Hebrew *lēb* is translated as heart, mind, and midst (Vine 1984, 177). The primary Greek word for heart is *kardia* (Vine 1984, 536). In Hebrew usage, the word heart was rarely used in the purely physical sense.

The ancient Hebrew "did not make a sharp distinction between physical and psychic powers and tended to attribute psychological functions to certain organs of the body" (Buttrick 1962, 549). The heart was viewed as the seat of psychic life. It was primarily the *mind* at its deepest level. This is the level Jesus Christ referred to when He replied, "Thou shalt love the Lord thy God with all thy heart, and with all thy soul, and with all thy mind" (Matthew 22:37; Deuteronomy 6:5) and when He said, "For out of the abundance of the heart the mouth speaketh" (Matthew 12:34). It is at this depth that we are who we really are, and it is out of this depth that the real us responds.

Heart is used first of man in Genesis 6:5: "And God saw that the wickedness of man was great in the earth, and that every imagination of the thoughts of his heart was only evil continually." Its second usage is in the verse that follows: "And it repented the Lord that he had made man on the earth, and it grieved him at his heart" (v. 6).

Generally speaking, the heart is "the home of the personal life." It is the sum total of who we are. If our human activity according to God's Word is wise, pure, upright, righteous, pious, and good, then our hearts are said to also be so (Easton 1897). On the other hand, if our activity is corrupt, rebellious, unrighteous, or destructive, then the heart is said to also be so.

The heart is described as the seat or center of man. It is the seat of emotions. The heart can be sad (Nehemiah 2:2), glad

*Seven Things God Hates*

(Proverbs 27:11), merry or sorrowful (Proverbs 15:13), troubled (2 Kings 6:11), envious (Proverbs 23:17), or trustful (Proverbs 31:11). The heart may be moved to hatred: "Do not hate a fellow Israelite in your heart" (Leviticus 19:17a). Conversely, the heart can love: "The Lord your God is testing you to find out whether you love him with all your heart and with all your soul" (Deuteronomy 13:3b). Whatever emotional state we are in, it springs from the heart.

The heart is also the seat of the intellect. The method of cogitation, thoughts, and meditation takes place in the heart. In Mark 2:6, the Pharisees are found reasoning in their hearts against the actions of Jesus (also see 1 Chronicles 29:18; Psalm 4:4). "As a man thinketh in his heart, so is he" (Proverbs 23:7). "Delight thyself also in the Lord; and he shall give thee the desires of thine heart" (Psalm 37:4).

In addition, the heart is viewed as the seat of volition (will) and the moral life of a person. The heart may be perverted (Proverbs 11:20), and it can be wicked (Matthew 15:19). It may be lifted in pride (Deuteronomy 8:14), and it may become hardened (Zechariah 7:12; Matthew 19:8), stubborn (Jeremiah 3:17), or godless (Psalm 14:1). In addition, man may have a good heart—one that is perfect (1 Kings 8:61), blameless (Psalm 119:80), clean (Psalm 51:10), honest and good (Luke 8:15), or pure (Matthew 5:18).

Finally, the heart is the seat of conscience. It is able to bear witness with God's Law (Romans 2:15). Most importantly, the heart is known to God, and if renewed, the heart is subject to God's influence, and He will allow His Word to dwell in the heart: "No, the word is very near you; it is in your mouth and in your heart so you may obey it" (Deuteronomy 30:14). By our own volition, we can hide God's Word in our hearts: "I have hidden your word in my heart that I might not sin against you" (Psalm 119:11). That same heart speaks to God (Psalm 27:8) and trusts Him (Psalm 28:7). God looks upon the heart (1 Samuel 16:7), knows its secrets (Psalm 44:21; Acts 1:24), and can harden the heart (Exodus 4:21) but also can turn it to good (Ezra 6:22).

As God can influence the heart of man to do good, Satan has similar power to influence the heart to do evil. There are only two influential spirits in the world: the Spirit to do that which is *godly* and the spirit to do that which is *ungodly*.

Judas experienced Satan's influence and betrayed the Lord for thirty pieces of silver, and Peter, who was sifted by the devil, thus succumbed three times to denial of Jesus (John 13:2; Matthew 26:69–75).

> There are only two influential spirits in the world: the Spirit to do that which is *godly* and the spirit to do that which is *ungodly*.

Both Ananias and Sapphira, while under Satan's influence, were inspired to lie to the Holy Spirit, an act that cost them their lives (Acts 5ff). When the believer's heart is opened to the power of the devil, we are easily deceived to act accordingly. To yield to the influence of the devil is to run afoul of the Spirit of God.

The influence of the Spirit on the heart is always present, urging man to return to God in a loving and intimate relationship. So is the influence of the devil on the heart of man. He is intent on turning man's heart away from God and completely destroying the relationship. In the end, those to whom we turn over our hearts and allow to sit on the throne of our hearts will determine the activities of the heart.

> Those to whom we turn over our hearts and allow to sit on the throne of our hearts will determine the activities of the heart.

*Seven Things God Hates*

The second word of interest is *devise*. In the original language, it is *charash*. It means to cut in, plough, engrave, and devise. It is used in Proverbs 3:29, wherein one is warned not to devise evil against a neighbor. It is used in Proverbs 6:14 with regard to a person who devises evil continually, and it is used in Proverbs 14:22 to describe both an individual who goes astray by devising evil and one who devises good and thus finds love and faithfulness (Young 1980, 253).

The third term is *imaginations*, or *schemes*, as found in the New International Version (NIV) of the Bible; it literally means "thought" and "device." In the Revised Standard Version (RSV), it is more accurately translated as "plan" and "device." Wicked schemes or wicked imaginations can also be translated as "thoughts of iniquity." The translation of imagination varies, but the intended meaning is "a heart that conjures up evil" (Young 1980, 509). Besides Proverbs 6:18, it is used in Lamentations 3:60: "Thou hast seen all their vengeance and all their imagination against me."

*Heart, deviseth,* and *wicked imagination*—of these four words, wicked is the term that brings condemnation. Man devises in his heart which action he will take, and of course there is nothing wrong or ungodly with planning or devising because God has endowed us with these abilities. But when we plan, plot, and scheme in our hearts to do evil, it signifies a depraved condition to which God says, "I hate it."

A wicked imagination is in rebellion against God, and it seeks to satisfy and indulge self at any cost. James pointed out, "What causes fights and quarrels among you? Don't they come from your desires that battle within you? You desire but do not have, so you kill. You covet but you cannot get what you want, so you quarrel and fight"

> A wicked imagination is in rebellion against God, and it seeks to satisfy and indulge self at any cost.

49

*Dr. Clarence Talley Sr.*

(James 4:1–2b). Imagination is a wonderful thing as long as it is aligned with the will of God. Unfortunately, as the Bible reveals, David imagined having Bathsheba, Uriah's wife (2 Samuel 11). Saul imagined having the booty of the Amalekites (1 Samuel 15:1–22). King Ahab imagined having Naboth's vineyard (1 Kings 21:1–13). James and John imagined calling down fire on the Samaritan village (Luke 9:51–56). The rich fool imagined building bigger barns (Luke 12:16–21), and Judas imagined having more money (John 12:6; Matthew 26:15).

Recent acts also reveal the wickedness of imagination and how far some are willing go to achieve horrific ends:

- It takes a wicked imagination to drown one's own children and then claim they were kidnapped.
- It takes a wicked imagination to lace letters with poison and send them through the United States postal system.
- It takes a wicked imagination to commandeer airplanes filled with people and then slam those planes into buildings filled with people.
- It takes a wicked imagination to rob long-time employees of their retirement nest egg.
- It takes a wicked imagination to drive around undetected, using military-style sniper equipment to kill innocent, unsuspecting citizens.
- It takes a wicked imagination to ordain leaders in the church whose lifestyle is contrary to the Word of God.
- It takes a wicked imagination to strap explosives to oneself and intentionally detonate those explosives, thus destroying oneself and others.
- It takes a wicked imagination to sit through a prayer meeting with others who are believers and then open fire on them, killing the pastor and nine others.
- It takes a wicked imagination to go into a church during worship service, open fire on worshippers, and slaughter more than two dozen people.

*Seven Things God Hates*

It should not be surprising what hearts fueled by wicked imaginations are willing to do. When the heart becomes a workshop for satanic activities, and Satan and his demons are allowed to sit on the workbench of your heart, he will, according to the apostle Paul, darken your understanding, thereby leaving you alienated from God and ignorant and blind in your heart. A darkened understanding that is ignorant and alienated from God sets the stage for an imagination willing to commit all kinds of unspeakable evil. Indeed, everything that comes out of the devil's workshop leads to death and destruction (Ephesians 4:18; Romans 1:21). Don't play with the devil's toys. Covetousness (2 Peter 2:14), lust (Proverbs 6:25), pride (Jeremiah 49:16), and rebellion (Jeremiah 5:23) are Satan's tools. He never has and never will construct anything that honors God. Out of Satan's workshop come "evil thoughts, murder, adultery, sexual immorality, theft, false testimony, slander" and a host of other things that are not pleasing to God and are destructive to man (Matthew 15:19; Galatians 5:19–22; Proverbs 14:12).

> Everything that comes out of the devil's workshop leads to death and destruction

On the other hand, a heart that knows God will "cast down imaginations, and every high thing that exalts itself against the knowledge of God, and bring into captivity every thought to the obedience of Christ" (2 Corinthians 10:5). A heart that knows God will devise to do His will. A heart that knows God will not seek to carry out the wicked activities of the imagination. The writer of Proverbs claimed, "Do not they err

> God did not create us to be brewers of evil plans in our hearts.

51

*Dr. Clarence Talley Sr.*

that devise evil? But mercy and truth shall be to them that devise good" (Proverbs 14:22).

God did not create us to be brewers of evil plans in our hearts. He created us to bring glory, honor, and praise to His name. Since God knows our hearts and knows to what extent they will yield evil if not committed to Him, we should commit our hearts to Him and plead, like David, "Create in me a clean heart, O God; and renew the right spirit with me" (Psalm 51:10).

God already has promised to give us new hearts. He said, "I will give you a new heart and put a new spirit in you; I will remove from you your heart of stone and give you a heart of flesh. And I will put my Spirit in you and move you to follow my decrees and be careful to keep my laws" (Ezekiel 36:26–27 NIV). God is saying in this passage that He will fix your heart, change your heart, renew your heart, and give you His Spirit, which will provide you with the necessary power to live in accordance to His laws.

God's Spirit will enable us to apply our hearts to understanding. He will also keep our hearts with all diligence and empower us to trust Him with all our hearts. As new creatures in Christ, with brand-new hearts, there will be no room for "a heart that devises wicked imaginations." Remember, only the pure in heart shall see God.

## Chapter 5 Study Questions

1. What is the condition of man's heart, according to Genesis 8:21 and Jeremiah 17:9?

2. The ancient Hebrew viewed the heart as the seat of _____. It was primarily the *mind* at its _____ level. Give an example.

3. What is meant by the phrase, the heart is "the home of the personal life"?

4. The heart is the seat of _____, _____, _____, and _____.

5. By our own volition, we can _____ God's Word in our _____.

6. Besides God, who else can influence our hearts?

*Dr. Clarence Talley Sr.*

7. How are the activities of the heart determined?

8. What are the warnings of Proverbs 3:29 and Proverbs 6:14?

9. When we plan, plot, and scheme in our hearts to do evil, it signifies a _____.

10. Imagination is a wonderful thing, as long as it is aligned with the _____.

11. List two biblical characters whose imaginations led to unholy acts.

12. List two recent acts from today's headlines that seemingly are rooted in wicked imaginations.

*Seven Things God Hates*

13. Everything that comes out of the devil's workshop leads to _____.

14. According to 2 Corinthians 10:5, what will a heart that knows God do with evil imaginations?

15. What is the cry of David in Psalm 51:10?

# 6

# FEET THAT BE SWIFT IN RUNNING TO MISCHIEF

Pride, lying, and murder preceded a heart that deviseth wicked imaginations, which is now followed by "feet that be swift in running to mischief." Like haughty eyes, a lying tongue, and hands that shed innocent blood, the feet are enthusiastic accomplices in the crimes of the heart. Whatever is devised in the workshop of the heart, swift feet willingly carry out. They anxiously await the mischievous instructions from the heart to fulfill whatever is the heart's purpose.

> Whatever is devised in the workshop of the heart, swift feet willingly carry out.

In this chapter, we will examine "feet that be swift in running to mischief" or, as the New International Version translates, "feet that are quick to rush into evil" (Proverbs 6:18b). This is the fifth thing in this passage that God declares He hates.

Feet completely support the weight of our bodies, but they also serve another major purpose, which is to assist in mobility. In cooperation with the legs, the feet transport us from one place to another. They may accomplish this by walking, running, or jogging. Without the feet, mobility is sorely impeded, and daily

*Seven Things God Hates*

activities are hindered. Thus, the feet are important; more important is how we use them.

Like the eyes (a proud look), the hands (hands that shed innocent blood), and the heart (a heart that devises evil), the feet also can be used to commit evil or to do good. They can be used to "flee youthful lust" (2 Timothy 2:22); avoid temptation, as Joseph did (Genesis 39); and to walk in worthiness and in love (Ephesians 4:1–3; 5:8). Conversely, the feet can be used to "walk in darkness" (Ecclesiastes 2:14) or "walk in the imagination of an evil heart" (Jeremiah 16:12), or they simply can be used to avoid doing what is right, as seen in the parable of the Good Samaritan (Luke 10:30–35).

In addition, the feet can be controlled and maneuvered in a variety of ways. They can move slowly or swiftly, carefully or neglectfully, purposefully or aimlessly, and reluctantly or willingly.

More specifically, what does the Bible have to say about this important organ? The Bible uses the word *feet* both literally and symbolically. The Lord said to Joshua, prior to possessing the land of Canaan, "I will give you every place you set your feet" (Joshua 1:3). The Lord's declaration was a symbol of *possession*. Joshua's obedient walk and trust in God after taking over leadership behind Moses would assure Israel's success in conquering the Promised Land.

To fall at another's feet was a symbol of *humility*. For instance, the leper cleansed by Jesus returned to Him "and fell down on his face at his feet, giving thanks" (Luke. 17:16). The Syrophoenician mother seeking help for her daughter also fell at the feet of Jesus in humility (Mark 7:25).

To kiss the feet was a symbol of *reverence*. The female sinner at Simon's house is said to have kissed the feet of Jesus. While Jesus ate, she "brought an alabaster box of ointment, And stood at his feet behind him weeping, and began to wash his feet with tears, and did wipe them with the hairs of her head, and kissed his feet, and anointed them with the ointment" (Luke 7:37–38).

Furthermore, the removal of the shoes from the feet was

*Dr. Clarence Talley Sr.*

symbolic of God's holiness and presence. On Mount Sinai, Moses was told by the voice in the burning bush to remove his shoes. "Do not come any closer," God said, "Take off your sandals, for the place you are standing is holy ground" (Exodus 3:5). To put under the feet symbolized conquest and subjugation of the enemy (Joshua 10:24; Psalm 110:1). Other symbolic activities involved the feet as well: Shaking the dust off of them was a sign of rejection (Matthew 10:14); washing of the feet was an act of hospitality (Luke. 7:4); and "to plunge your feet in the blood of your foes" was a symbol of victory.

Feet that are swift in running to mischief is symbolic of a person's rushing to do evil—hence, the translation "feet that are quick to rush into evil." The Hebrew word for swift is *mahar*, which means "to hasten." We don't rush to do those activities that we consider unimportant, but we do those things we are anxious about doing without delay. The urgency to do things that are destructive, negative, or hurtful reveals the grave condition of the heart that guides the feet.

> The urgency to do things that are destructive, negative, or hurtful reveals the grave condition of the heart that guides the feet.

For example, in Genesis 37, Joseph's brothers moved swiftly against him because their hearts were already set on harming their brother. Their hearts had been meditating negatively on Joseph ("the dreamer"). Notice how the condition of their hearts is revealed in their words.

Joseph had been sent by Israel, their father, to check on his brothers' condition as they managed the flocks in the fields (Genesis 37:12–13). As Joseph approached them in the grazing plains near Dothan, the brothers saw him coming in the distance, "and before he reached them, they plotted to kill him" (Genesis 37:18). They said, "Here comes the dreamer!" to

*Seven Things God Hates*

each other. "Come now, let's kill him and throw him into one of these cisterns and say [to our father Israel] that a ferocious animal devoured him. Then we'll see what come of his dreams" (vv. 19–20).

Seemingly without much thought, Joseph's brothers swiftly acted against him. Their hands and feet complied with the condition of their hearts, and Joseph, the beloved son of their father, was quickly done away with (Genesis 37:21–30)—or so they believed (Genesis 45).

Another example of feet that are quick to rush into evil is found in the person of Jezebel. In 1 Kings 21, Jezebel moved swiftly against Naboth to secure his vineyard for her husband, King Ahab. On trumped-up charges, she had Naboth accused of cursing God and the king. She had false witnesses testify against him. As a result, Naboth was found guilty and then stoned to death.

On another occasion, though this time without success, Jezebel also acted swiftly against the prophet Elijah, who had killed 450 of her false prophets. She threatened to see to it that within twenty-four hours, Elijah would meet with a tragic end. She said, "May the gods deal with me, be it ever so severely, if by this time tomorrow I do not make your life like that of one of them" (1 Kings 19:1–2).

Today, people are still swift to engage in evil. From first-degree murder, to sexual assault, to robbery, to drugs, to prostitution, to violent street protests, the statistics show that humans' feet are busily involved in the works of the devil. Even in activities where no legal actions are taken and no formal empirical data are kept, people openly and privately participate. They engage in activities such as adultery, fornication, gambling, promiscuity, lying, slander, gossip, and drunkenness, all of which are an abomination to God and, moreover, lead to destruction. Motivated by a bad heart, the feet move quickly to fulfill desires contrary to Christian living.

Those who rush headlong into evil will pay. The warning is simple: "There is a way that seemeth right unto a man, but the

*Dr. Clarence Talley Sr.*

end thereof are the ways of death" (Proverbs 14:12). The wages of sin have not changed. "For the wages of sin is death, but the gift of God is eternal life in Christ Jesus our Lord" (Romans. 6:23). Consequently, one must guard against letting the feet stray onto the wrong path, follow the wrong crowd, or stand in the wrong place.

> One must guard against letting the feet stray onto the wrong path, follow the wrong crowd, or stand in the wrong place.

In warning his son to keep his feet clear of evil activities and not be drawn in by the wrong crowd, whose feet are contaminated, Solomon advised, "My son, do not go along with them, do not set foot on their path; for their feet rush into sin, they are swift to shed blood" (Proverbs 1:15–16). Furthermore, Solomon advised, "Make level paths for your feet and take only the ways that are firm. Do not swerve to the right or the left; keep your foot from evil" (Proverbs 4:26–27). Obviously, Solomon offered good advice, but good advice is not always heeded. Unfortunately, in 1 Kings 12:6–15, King Rehoboam, Solomon's son, "forsook the counsel of the old men, which they had given him, and consulted with the young men that were grown up with him." Rehoboam's acceptance of bad counsel from his peers plunged the nation into chaos.

Centuries later, Jesus Christ gave a warning regarding the paths our feet are subject to take. He said, "Enter ye in at the strait gate: for wide is the gate, and broad is the way, that leadeth to destruction, and many there be which go in thereat. Because strait is the gate, and narrow is the way, which leadeth unto life, and few there be that find it" (Matthew 7:13–14).

The first path is broad and leads to destruction; the second path is narrow and leads to life. Jesus explained that few feet are found trampling the narrow path, but many feet are found on the broad path. The warning here, as it was from Solomon, is also to "keep your feet from evil" by taking the right path, which is clearly identified by Jesus as the narrow path.

The psalmist confessed, "I have kept my feet from every evil path so that I might obey your word" (Psalm 119:101). Feet kept from evil are obedient feet. They are feet that seek to do God's will. They are feet that find their way through the "strait gate" and onto the narrow way. To this end, obedient feet are kept by God and directed by God. They are feet that "depart from evil, and do good; seek peace, and pursue it" (Psalm 34:14).

> Obedient feet are kept by God and directed by God.

Psalm 37:23–24 proclaims this fact: "The steps of a good man are ordered by the Lord: and he delighted in his way." Moreover, God's Word serves as a lamp and a light to one's pathway, leads obedient feet in paths of righteousness, keeps obedient feet from slipping, and directs obedient feet in the way they should go (Psalm 119:105; 23:3; 66:9; Isaiah 48:17).

Conversely, the feet of the disobedient are an abomination to the Lord. They operate and move on a whim. They have no sense of direction, morally or spiritually. They are always prone to the wrong direction. They prefer to stand in the counsel of others who are disobedient (Psalm 1:1), and they "walk in ways of darkness" (Proverbs 2:13).

The use of our appendages for acts of unrighteousness was emphatically denounced by the apostle Paul. He argued that because of what Christ did, sin no longer has dominion in the body. It is freed from sin. Its members are

> Will we permit our feet to be the flunky of the heart, its partner in crime, carrying out its evil desires?

now dead to sin and alive to Christ (Romans 6:1–11). Paul commanded, "Let not sin therefore reign in your mortal body, that ye should obey it in the lusts thereof. Neither yield ye your members as instruments of unrighteousness unto sin: but yield yourselves unto God, as those who are alive from the dead, and your members as instruments of righteousness unto God" (Romans 6:12–13).

In conclusion, our feet are important, but how we use them is most important. Shall we use them as instruments of righteousness, as Paul commands, or as instruments of unrighteousness, which he rejects? Will we allow our feet to be enthusiastic accomplices of evil, or will we use them for the glory of God? Will we permit our feet to be the flunky of the heart, its partner in crime, carrying out its evil desires? Will we allow our feet to have their own way? Or will we subject our feet to the ways of God?

> Christian feet should hold all the world records for sprinting in love, joy, peace, kindness, and sacrifice.

The feet of the Christian must be consecrated, dedicated, and fully committed to the ways of God. We must have "feet that are swift in running to righteousness." They must be feet that are swift to visit the sick, the shut-ins, and those in prison. In track and field terms, Christian feet should hold all the world records for sprinting in love, joy, peace, kindness, and sacrifice:

- Christian feet should be faster than Carl Lewis in displaying the love of God.
- Christian feet should be swifter than Michael Johnson in reconciling broken relationships.
- Christian feet should be quicker than Usain Bolt in forgiving an erring brother, faltering sister, unfaithful

*Seven Things God Hates*

spouse, or prodigal son (Matthew 5:23–24; Ephesians 4:32; Luke 15:11ff).

- Every Christian should have feet like those of Gail Devers—feet that are swift in leaping hurdles or barriers to share the Word of God with others.
- Christian feet must move at world-record pace, compelling others to come in and have their feet washed in the blood of the Lamb (Matthew 28:19–20).

The God who hates feet that are swift to rush into evil also declares, "How beautiful are the feet of those who bring good news!" On earth, Christians serve as the "feet" of Jesus Christ. Let Him use yours.

## Chapter 6 Study Questions

1. The feet can be used to commit _____ or to do _____.

2. What are some ways the feet can be used?

3. List and explain three symbolic uses of the feet.

4. The urgency to do things that are _____, _____, or _____ reveals the grave condition of the _____ that guides the _____.

5. Cite a New Testament example of feet that be swift in running to mischief.

6. Explain the warning of Proverbs 14:12.

*Seven Things God Hates*

7. What is the advice of Solomon to his son regarding his feet and the path they take?

8. What path in life does Jesus recommend to believers?

9. Obedient feet are _____ by God and _____ by God.

10. Paul recommended that we use our members, body parts, as instruments of _____.

11. Christian feet should hold all the world records for sprinting in _____, in _____,in_____, in _____, and in _____.

# 7

# A FALSE WITNESS THAT SPEAKETH LIES

Because of the indiscretion of William Jefferson Clinton, former president of the United States of America, world attention for a time became focused on the issue of lying and false testimony. Never in recent years had such acts been so hotly argued, debated, and discussed. Legal experts, moral activists, and the politically motivated climbed on either the bandwagon of denunciation or the bandwagon of acceptance. Some said, "It's not a big deal," while others found the president's behavior reprehensible. Everyone had an opinion about what constitutes sex, what is truth, and what should be done to the holder of the highest office in the free world.

Man's opinion, however, doesn't really matter. It didn't matter then and still doesn't matter today because centuries ago, the issue was settled with the ninth commandment of the Decalogue, which states, "Thou shalt not bear false witness against thy neighbor" (Exodus 20:16).

The God of truth condemns false testimony and lying. Accordingly, His disgust of a "false witness that speaketh lies" is number six among the things God hates (Proverbs 6:19a).

We have already commented on a lying tongue, the second element in this series. Here, however, we examine a particular aspect under which lying is regarded. Bearing false witness refers more so to lying in a court of law while under oath.

Also known as perjury, lying under oath subsequently erodes the effectiveness of a society's judicial system. Therefore, to assure each individual fair treatment and an honest trial, our laws are designed to deal harshly with those who lie under oath. Truthfulness is commanded by God and required by just men.

Lying is the willful perversion of the truth with the intent to deceive. It is one of the more destructive sins of the tongue, whether in or out of the courtroom, board room, or bedroom. An individual may lie boldly, evasively, silently, or hypocritically. In other words, a lie can be said or unsaid. By some standards, truth politely avoided is a lie. A person can keep quiet and still lie. And a life lived as a charade is also a lie.

Lying is destructive and deadly because it undermines the social fabric of the community and nation. It also reveals a hatred for God and man.

Lying, as we have learned, is satanically inspired. Its inventor is the devil, the father of lies. Satan and his demons work to sow lies among men, and anyone who bears false witness, speaks lies, or practices deceit is also in his employ.

While speaking to the Pharisees, Jesus said, "You belong to your father, the devil, and you want to carry out your father's desires. He was a murderer from the beginning, not holding to the truth, for there is no truth in him" (John 8:44). Therefore, every lie is satanically inspired. Again, it originates with the devil in the cavern of the heart.

> **Truthfulness is commanded by God and required by just men.**

> **Lying is destructive and deadly because it undermines the social fabric of the community and nation.**

*Dr. Clarence Talley Sr.*

As a result, the heart is the birthplace of lying and other abominations. "For out of the heart come evil thoughts—murder, adultery, sexual immorality, theft, false testimony, slander" (Matthew 15:19). It is out of the abundance of the heart that the tongue, "an unruly evil full of deadly poison," speaks (Matthew 12:34; James 3:8). It is out of the heart that lying lips get their directives.

> Integrity in speech has long since become an ancient art—a lost practice.

Nowadays, truth is no longer regarded as the bedrock of society. Expediency is the order of the day. If bearing false witness and speaking lies promotes one's agenda, then so be it. If approaching truth subjectively and relatively will gain for some the desires of their hearts, then so be it.

For most, integrity in speech has long since become an ancient art—a lost practice. And like so many things pertaining to God and godliness, truthful speech is now a cheap commodity. Telling the truth, the whole truth, and nothing but the truth is viewed as optional. The mantra "what is truth for you may not be truth for me" rings loudly in public discourse. In the world of business, in the political arena, even in our churches and personal lives, honesty and truthfulness have become of little or no importance.

> The act of placing one's hand on the Bible and swearing to tell the truth but then lying is seen as "no big deal."

The act of placing one's hand on the Bible and swearing to tell the truth but then lying is seen as "no big deal." Once upon a time, a man's word was his bond, and a handshake sealed the deal because it was held as a sacred trust.

*Seven Things God Hates*

Besides the ninth commandment, "You shall not give false testimony against your neighbor," the Israelites were warned several times in the Pentateuch and in the wisdom literature against such behavior. Here are some other reminders found in scripture:

"Thou shalt not raise a false report: put not thine hand with the wicked to be an unrighteous witness" (Exodus 23:1). "A false witness shall not be unpunished, and he that speaketh lies shall not escape" (Proverbs 19:5). "A man that beareth false witness against his neighbor is a maul, and a sword, and a sharp arrow" (Proverbs 25:18).

In short, the Israelites were counseled to not testify falsely because they would not get away with it, no matter how much injury they inflicted on a neighbor.

Even with these warnings, false witnesses rose among the Hebrew community (Psalm 27:12; 35:11). As a result, the Lord methodically spelled out for the people how to handle a false witness once they were discovered. God says,

> If a malicious witness comes forward and accuses someone of a crime, then both the accuser and accused must appear before the Lord by coming to the priests and judges in office at that time. The judges must investigate the case thoroughly. If the accuser has brought false charges against his fellow Israelite, you must impose on the accuser the sentence he intended for the other person. In this way, you will purge such evil from among you. Then the rest of the people will hear about it and be afraid to do such an evil thing. You must show no pity for the guilty! Your rule should be life for life, eye for eye, tooth for tooth, hand for hand, foot for foot. (Deuteronomy 19:16–21 NLT)

As you can see, a false witness in the community was not to be taken lightly. If a malicious witness accused a man of a crime, the two men involved in the dispute had to stand in the presence of the Lord before the priest and the judges who were in office at the time. The judges had to make a thorough investigation. If the witness proved to be a liar, having given false testimony against his brother, then the priests and the judges were to do to him as he intended to do to his brother. In doing so, the evil from among the people would be removed. The end result was that the remaining people would hear of it and be afraid, and never again would such an evil thing be done among the people.

God made it very clear how to handle a false witness when discovered. He was deeply concerned about the effect this evil had on the Hebrew community, and it is evident in the severity of the punishment mentioned: "Show no pity: life for life, eye for eye, tooth for tooth, hand for hand, foot for foot" (Deuteronomy 19:21). Perjury—false testimony—was to be dealt with to the fullest extent of the Mosaic Law.

To further ward off injury to the innocent, the Law required two or more witnesses before convicting someone. No one was to be found guilty or put to death on the testimony of only one witness. "One witness shall not rise up against a man for any iniquity, or for any sin, in any sin that he sinneth: at the mouth of two witnesses, or at the mouth of three witnesses, shall the matter be established" (Deuteronomy 19:15). This admonition is repeated in other places. "At the mouth of two witnesses, or three witnesses, shall he that is worthy of death be put to death; but at the mouth of one witness he shall not be put to death" (Deuteronomy 17:6; Numbers 35:30). The judicial procedure is cogent. More than one witness is always required.

Notorious behind-the-scene activities, however, even with two or more witnesses, still led to the persecution and death of innocent victims. For example, in the case of Naboth and his vineyard, Queen Jezebel bribed two witnesses to falsely accuse Naboth in order to gain his vineyard for her covetous, sulking husband, King Ahab (1 Kings 21).

Further, in the trial of Jesus Christ, witnesses whose

*Seven Things God Hates*

testimonies did not agree were sought and brought in by the chief priest to testify against Him. "And the chief priests and all the council sought for witness against Jesus to put him to death; and found none. For many bare false witness against him, but their witness agreed not together" (Mark 14:55–56ff).

The travesty committed against the Joseph of the Old Testament was based on the testimony of one pagan witness. It was Joseph's word against Potiphar's wife, who falsely accused him of rape. In the end, Joseph was not believed, and as a result he was thrown into prison (Genesis 39:7ff).

The New Testament also commands not to witness falsely against one's neighbor. Jesus replied, "You shall not murder, you shall not commit adultery, you shall not steal, you shall not give false testimony" (Matthew 19:18; Mark 10:19; Luke 18:20; Romans 13:9).

Truthfulness of testimony, therefore, is stressed, and the practice of establishing guilt by two or more witnesses also is instituted. It is reiterated in Matthew 18:16, where an erring brother refuses to listen to another who addresses him in love. The advice of scripture is to go to him a second time, taking another witness. "That in the mouth of two or three witnesses every word may be established."

The apostle Paul also mentions this concept in dealing with the Corinthian church. "This is the third time I am coming to you. In the mouth of two or three witnesses shall every word be established" (2 Corinthians. 13:1). Problems in the Corinthian church would be dealt with upon Paul's return to Corinth, but it would be dealt with according to the Mosaic Law; no one could be condemned on the evidence of one witness (Deuteronomy 19:15).

Paul also charges the youthful pastor Timothy to make use of the same procedure when accusations are brought to him by one church member against another. "Do not entertain an accusation against an elder unless it is brought by two or three witnesses" (1 Timothy 5:19).

Much of what is said about church leaders and lay members

could be quickly laid to rest if the church today practiced Paul's advice. The testimony of one person must be corroborated by another. Certainly, there would be fewer hurt feelings, church fights, and church splits.

Finally, we are warned against bearing false witness and speaking lies, whether publicly or privately. In Matthew 11:18–19, false accusations against John the Baptist and Jesus are mentioned by the Master. "For John came neither eating nor drinking, and they say, 'He has a demon.' The Son of Man came eating and drinking, and they say, 'Here is a glutton and a drunkard, a friend of tax collectors and sinners.' But wisdom is proved right by her deeds."

Furthermore, speaking falsely, privately, or secretly against others is an insult to God. To do so even covertly is warned against. God has declared, "Whoever slanders their neighbor in secret, I will put to silence; whoever has haughty eyes and a proud heart, I will not tolerate" (Psalm 101:5).

Secret defamation is appalling to God. It is an attack against an individual's character and property. So-called white lies, half truths, or embellished falsehoods, spoken publicly or privately, can destroy what has taken a lifetime to build—a good name and a good reputation.

God, therefore, has promised to mete out the appropriate punishment to those who commit

> So-called white lies, half truths, or embellished falsehoods, spoken publicly or privately, can destroy what has taken a lifetime to build—a good name and a good reputation.

> "Stop your love for telling lies that you swear are the truth."

*Seven Things God Hates*

such evil. He has pledged to be a "swift witness" against "false swearers." He says, "So I will come to put you on trial. I will be quick to testify against sorcerers, adulterers, and perjurers" (Malachi 3:5). Additionally, the Lord vows, "A false witness will not go unpunished, and he who pours out lies will not go free" (Proverbs 19:5); "A false witness will perish" (Proverbs 21:28); and he will be banished from the presence of God (Zechariah 5:3–4; Revelation 21:8).

Emphatically and repeatedly, God says, "Do not testify against your neighbor without cause, or use your lips to deceive" (Proverbs 24:28). How much clearer can God be regarding this sixth evil that He hates? The Decalogue, the wisdom literature, and the New Testament all affirm the Lord's position. Unquestionably, the believer must heed and act. "Don't scheme against each other. Stop your love for telling lies that you swear are the truth. I hate all these things, says the Lord" (Zechariah 8:17).

## Chapter 7 Study Questions

1. What is the ninth commandment of the Decalogue?

2. Truthfulness is commanded by _____ and required by just _____.

3. _____ is the willful perversion of the truth with the intent to deceive.

4. The _____ is the birthplace of _____ and other abominations.

5. Complete the mantra: "What is truth for you _____."

6. In many of our courts today, what is now seen as "no big deal"?

7. How were false witnesses to be handled among the Israelites?

*Seven Things God Hates*

8. Two or more witnesses were needed to protect the _____.

9. What is the teaching of Deuteronomy 17:6?

10. According to Matthew 18:16, how is truthful testimony gained and guilt established?

11. In Matthew 11:18–19, false accusations against _____ and _____ are mentioned.

12. Speaking falsely, privately, or secretly against others is an _____ to God.

13. What will be the punishment for those who witness falsely and speak lies?

14. What is the warning of Proverbs 24:28?

15. Stop your _____ for telling _____ that you swear are the _____.

# 8

# HE THAT SOWETH DISCORD AMONG THE BRETHREN

The seventh and final act in the Proverbs passage that God so vociferously declares He hates is a man who stirs up dissension among the brothers (Proverb 6:19b). These are individuals who, for one reason or another, spend much of their energy causing confusion, stirring up a stinker, and influencing others to focus on the negative in order to create disagreement and division.

You will find them among the church and the world. People of this nature are messy troublemakers who find sparks of differences and dissatisfaction among individuals and fan them into flames of discord. They use a variety of methods to accomplish their task. They slander, lie, spread rumors, gossip, and start vain talk, just to name a few.

Every believer must be mindful of what he or she says and does, always controlling motivations that are not edifying to the body of Jesus Christ. We are all instruments in one of two camps: either good or evil. The apostle Paul warns us in that regard: "Therefore do not let sin reign in your mortal body so that you obey its evil desires. Do not offer any part of yourself to sin as an instrument of wickedness, but rather offer yourselves to God as those who have been brought from death to life; and offer every part of yourself to him as an instrument of righteousness" (Romans 6:12–13).

*Seven Things God Hates*

Everyone who sows seeds of discord has yielded to the works of unrighteousness and thus has become a tool for evil. They are inspired to destroy the peace among brothers, and often this inspiration grows out of hatred, pride, and/or self-righteousness. Paul said we must be careful to let "no division among us that we may be perfectly united in mind and thought" (1 Corinthians 1:10).

Any activity that jeopardizes the unity of the believers must be contained, or else, like a little leaven, it will ruin the entire body. "For where you have envy and selfish ambition, there you find disorder and every evil practice" (James 3:16). James warns that negative emotions, if not brought under control, will lead to all kinds of divisive and corrupt acts. To the person or persons who initiate such activity, God says, "I hate it."

Those who allow themselves to be used as agents of contention cause problems for themselves and others. Notice Solomon, the wise man, identifies many ways strife and division are stirred up among the brethren. He states the following: "An angry man stirs up dissension" (Proverbs 29:22); "Hatred stirs up dissension" (Proverbs 10:12); "Pride only breeds quarrels" (Proverbs 13:10); "A hot tempered man stirs up dissension" (Proverbs 15:18); "A perverse man stirs up dissension and gossip

> Everyone who sows seeds of discord has yielded to the works of unrighteousness and thus has become a tool for evil.

> Any activity that jeopardizes the unity of the believers must be contained, or else, like a little leaven, it will ruin the entire body.

separates close friends" (Proverbs 16:28); and "A fool's lips bring him strife, and his mouth invites beatings" (Proverbs 18:6).

Anger, hatred, pride, perversion, and gossip are just some of the ways in which dissension can work its way into our lives. As a result, we must continually be on guard against such evils. Troublemakers in the church will reap the reward of their havoc. God will not be mocked. Whatever troublemakers sow, that shall they also reap. Solomon makes it plain: "It is to one's honor to avoid strife, but every fool is quick to quarrel" (Proverbs 20:3).

> "It is to one's honor to avoid strife, but every fool is quick to quarrel."

Avoidance was Abraham's solution to minimize strife and contention between him and his nephew Lot and their herdsmen. Abraham, then known as Abram, said to Lot, "Let's not have any quarreling between you and me, or between your herders and mine, for we are close relatives" (Genesis 13:8). Abraham was careful to maintain a balance of peace between him and others. Abraham understood that strife and division characterize the world but should not typify the family members of God.

> Love and unity must be the thread that binds the church.

Love and unity must be the thread that binds the church. The psalmist wrote, "How good and pleasant it is when brothers live together in unity" (Psalm 133:1). Those in the church who promote quarreling, outbursts of anger, factions, slander, discord, and dissension shall not inherit the kingdom of God. Paul argued that we are many members, yet we are one body—many parts but unified in Jesus Christ (1 Corinthians 12:20).

Likewise, the believer must follow after peace, not strife and

*Seven Things God Hates*

division. Paul contended that those who disrupt the unity of believers are to be avoided. He advised believers to "watch out for those who cause divisions and put obstacles in your way that are contrary to the teaching you have learned. Keep away from them" (Romans 16:17). The church at Philippi also received a stern warning against those who sought to disrupt, divide, and cause dissension. They were told to "watch out for those dogs." Guarding against such would assure the unity among believers.

Believers are to be mindful that "the one who is throwing you into confusion, whoever that may be, will have to pay the penalty" (Galatians 5:10). Those who purposely cause disruption to peace in the church will be dealt with harshly by the head of the church. It was David's prayer that God intercede on behalf of His people and deal severely with the sowers of discord. David prayed, "Repay them for their deeds and for their evil work; repay them for what their hands have done and bring back upon them what they deserve" (Psalm 28:4 NIV).

Thus, Christians must be peacemakers and not peace breakers. It is our Christian duty to "do everything without grumbling or arguing, so that you may become blameless and pure, children of God without fault in a warped and crooked generation" (Philippians 2:14–15b).

The family of God is characterized by peace. At all costs, they are to avoid "strife, abusive language, evil suspicions and constant friction between men" (1 Timothy 6:4–5) because "those who practice such things shall not inherit the kingdom of God" (Galatians 5:21). Jesus Christ has left us with His peace—peace the world cannot give or take away. "Peace I leave with you; my peace I give you. I do not give to you as the world gives. Do not let your heart be troubled and do not be afraid" (John 14:27 NIV).

> Christians must be peacemakers and not peace breakers.

In a world where disunity seems unavoidable, the badge of

*Dr. Clarence Talley Sr.*

the Christian must be one of peace and unity. Jesus Christ is the Prince of Peace. God the Father is not a God of chaos. Therefore, the Christian life must reflect the serenity that flows from the guidance of the Holy Spirit in every way. Remember: God hates "a man who stirs up dissension among brothers," but "blessed are the peacemakers for they will be called the sons of God" (Matthew 5:9).

## Chapter 8 Study Questions

1. What are some of the ways the flames of discord may be spread among believers?

2. Everyone who sows seeds of discord has yielded to the works of _____.

3. List several of the agents of contention and strife, as identified by Solomon.

4. How did Abraham minimize strife between him and his nephew Lot?

5. _____ and _____ must be the thread that binds the _____.

6. What was Paul's warning to the Philippian church?

*Dr. Clarence Talley Sr.*

7. What did David want done to those who purposely caused disruption in the church?

8. Christians must be _____ and not _____.

9. The Christian life must reflect the _____ that flows from the guidance of the _____.

# CONCLUDING THOUGHTS

Proverbs 6:17–19 clearly states seven particular things God hates. We began by trying to understand why the God of love would express Himself in this manner. We've learned that God's hatred of sin and certain types of people is *not* contrary to His character. As a God of love, anything that is opposed to His love is sin, and anyone who is given over to the evils we have discussed is an abomination in His sight.

God's hatred is an expression of His opposition to sin, as well as His love for the sinner. Again, only God can love perfectly and hate perfectly. The seven things that God has specifically highlighted in this passage are sins that easily beset all of us—sins that the apostle Paul encourages believers to lay aside and do away with (Hebrew 12:1). As believers, we must be sensitive to God's abhorrence for such evils, avoid becoming entangled in them, and be merciful—with all diligence—to those who are ensnared. It is our solemn duty to come to the aid of others, for as we have received our strength, we must work to strengthen our brothers.

> God's hatred is an expression of His opposition to sin, as well as His love for the sinner.

Jude offers these words of advice to believers in their dealings with sinners, for whom Jesus Christ died: "Be merciful to those who doubt; save others by snatching them from the fire; to others show mercy, mixed with fear—hating even the clothing stained by corrupted flesh" (Jude 1:22–23). Evil deeds are to be hated in a manner that motivates us to help and rescue. To the church at Ephesus, Jesus acknowledged their hatred of evil deeds—deeds He also hated: "But you have this in your favor: You hate the practices of the Nicolaitanes, which I also hate" (Revelation 2:6).

> To hate the sin, to love the sinner, and to be merciful to all are acts of compassion.

The apostle Paul also advised that our mission to assist others must always be done in love and meekness. We are to hate what is sinful. On the other hand, we must seek to help our fallen brother. We are to "speak the truth in love," walk wisely before men, and come humbly to the aid of those in need. Our love for others, according to Jesus, must be extended even to our enemies (Ephesians 5:15; Galatians 6:1–2; Matthew 5:44).

To hate the sin, to love the sinner, and to be merciful to all are acts of compassion. To hate what God hates is to love what and who God loves and to share His love with everyone with whom we come in contact. The believer's abhorrence for evil reflects the fatherhood of God, an image the world needs to see.

We have learned that hate that is motivated by godly love and compassion is a holy hatred. A godly disdain for evil must have its roots in a holy God and be sustained by the power of the Spirit of God.

> Hatred that promotes destruction, division, and death dishonors God.

In fact, we have learned that what God opposes is what believers are to rightfully oppose in the power of His might. We must always remember, however, that as children of God, all that we do must "be done decently and in order." Hate that is motivated by an ungodly spirit, a spirit of ulterior motives, or a spirit of destruction brings judgment and condemnation from God.

A holy dislike that engages and encourages the best in a person, while deploring the worst, benefits everyone, but hatred that promotes destruction, division, and death dishonors God. It is a sin and, in some instances, a crime. We are *not* commanded by the God of love to hate absolutely or maliciously. Hate of this type is unholy and only leads to acts of man's inhumanity to man, as we have witnessed throughout the course of human history.

The Christian's reaction to sin must mimic God's hatred for the same. Whether society accepts this perspective or not, believers must stand firm on the Word of God, knowing that if God is for us, He is more than the world, the flesh, and the devil against us. God loves us so much that He sent His Son to redeem us from the spirit that causes malicious actions toward one another.

> ## The Christian's reaction to sin must mimic God's hatred for the same.

Even when we fall short, God loves us so much that He will discipline us in love to bring us back to Him. "For the Lord disciplines the one He loves, and He chastises everyone He receives as a son" (Hebrews 12:6). Since God never gives up on us, we must never give up on each other. We must always mimic God in every way.

God is still saying, "I hate pride; it goes before destruction, and Satan is the architect.

"I hate lying; it perverts truth, and its intent is to deceive.

"I hate murder; it cuts off the crown of creation, and it is a crime against My image.

"I hate evil thoughts; they are birthed in the workshop of the devil.

"I hate unholy feet; they travel swiftly in ungodly directions to accomplish ungodly acts.

"I hate false witnesses; they ruin lives, destroy reputations, and erode the moral fiber of society.

"I hate dissension; it divides people and perpetuates strife."

God says, "I hate it. I hate it. I hate it!"

## APPENDIX

# FORTY-THREE THINGS GOD HATES

(From *Meredith's Book of Bible Lists*)

1. God hates homosexual acts (Leviticus 18:22).
2. God hates sexual acts between humans and animals (Leviticus 18:23).
3. God hates idols and even the precious metals and other materials which have been used in making idols (Deuteronomy 7:25).
4. God hates blemished sacrifices (Deuteronomy 17:1).
5. God hates the worship of the sun, moon, or stars (Deuteronomy 17:3, 4).
6. God hates divination (Deuteronomy 18:10).
7. God hates astrology (Deuteronomy 18:10).
8. God hates enchanters (Deuteronomy 18:10).
9. God hates witches (Deuteronomy 18:10).
10. God hates charmers (Deuteronomy 18:11).
11. God hates wizards (Deuteronomy 18:11).
12. God hates necromancers (Deuteronomy 18:11).
13. God hates the wearing of clothing of the opposite sex (Deuteronomy 22:5).
14. God hates and will not accept as an offering the hire of a whore (Deuteronomy 23:18 KJV).
15. God hates remarriage to a former wife after she has been married to another man (Deuteronomy 24:4).

16. God hates scales that are falsely calibrated to cheat the customer (Deuteronomy 25:13–16).
17. God hates the workers of iniquity (Psalm 5:5).
18. God hates the wicked (Psalm 11:5).
19. God hates those who love violence (Psalm 11:5).
20. God hates the forward [perverse] (Proverbs 3:32).
21. God hates a proud look (Proverbs 6:16, 17).
22. God hates a lying tongue (Proverbs 6:17).
23. God hates hands that shed innocent blood (Proverbs 6:17).
24. God hates a heart that devises wicked imaginations (Proverbs 6:18).
25. God hates feet that are swift in running to mischief (Proverbs 6:18).
26. God hates a false witness who speaks lies (Proverbs 6:19).
27. God hates anyone who sows discord among brethren (Proverbs 6:19).
28. God hates lying lips (Proverbs 12:22).
29. God hates the sacrifices of the wicked (Proverbs 15:8).
30. God hates the ways of the wicked (Proverbs 15:9).
31. God hates the thoughts of the wicked (Proverbs 15:26).
32. God hates the proud in heart (Proverbs 16:5).
33. God hates those who justify the wicked (Proverbs 17:15).
34. God hates those who condemn the just (Proverbs 17:15).
35. God hates vain sacrifices (Isaiah 1:13).
36. God hated the feasts of the new moon celebrated by the Hebrews during the days of Isaiah (Isaiah 1:14).
37. God hates robbery for burnt offering (Isaiah 61:8).
38. God hates idolatry (Jeremiah 44:2–4).
39. God hates evil plans against neighbors (Zechariah 8:17).
40. God hates false oaths (Zechariah 8:17).
41. God hated Esau (Malachi 1:1–3; Romans 9:13).
42. God hates divorce (Malachi 2:14–16).
43. God hates the deeds of the Nicolaitanes (Revelation 2:6).

*Two suggested additions to Meredith's List* (from livingtheway. org/43things.html) *are as follows:*

44. God hates sacred pillars (Deuteronomy 16:22).
45. God hates feast days (Amos 5:21).

## APPENDIX 2

# JESUS CHRIST'S USE OF THE WORD HATE

1.  Ye have heard that it hath been said, Thou shalt love thy neighbour, and hate thine enemy. But I say unto you, Love your enemies, bless them that curse you, do good to them that hate you, and pray for them which despitefully use you, and persecute you (Matthew 5:43–44).
2.  No man can serve two masters: for either he will hate the one, and love the other; or else he will hold to the one, and despise the other. Ye cannot serve God and mammon (Matthew 6:24).
3.  And then shall many be offended, and shall betray one another, and shall hate one another (Matthew 24:10).
4.  Blessed are ye, when men shall hate you, and when they shall separate you from their company, and shall reproach you, and cast out your name as evil, for the Son of man's sake (Luke 6:22).
5.  But I say unto you which hear, Love your enemies, do good to them which hate you (Luke 6:27).
6.  If any man come to me, and hate not his father, and mother, and wife, and children, and brethren, and sisters, yea, and his own life also, he cannot be my disciple (Luke 14:26).
7.  No servant can serve two masters: for either he will hate the one, and love the other; or else he will hold to the one,

and despise the other. Ye cannot serve God and mammon (Luke 16:13).

8. The world cannot hate you; but me it hateth, because I testify of it, that the works thereof are evil (John 7:7).
9. If the world hate you, ye know that it hated me before it hated you (John 15:18).
10. But this thou hast, that thou hatest the deeds of the Nicolaitanes, which I also hate (Revelation 2:6).
11. So hast thou also them that hold the doctrine of the Nicolaitanes, which thing I hate (Revelation 2:15).

# BIBLIOGRAPHY

Buttrick, G. A. *The Interpreter's Dictionary of the Bible*. New York: Abingdon Press, 1962.

Easton, M. A. *Illustrated Bible Dictionary*, 3rd ed. New York: Thomas Nelson, 1897.

Elwell, Walter A. *Baker Encyclopedia of the Bible*, vol. 1–2. Grand Rapids, Michigan: Baker Book House, 1988.

Harrison, R. K. *The Encyclopedia of Biblical Ethics*. New York: Thames Nelson, 1992.

Lockyer, Herbert Sr., ed. *Nelson's Illustrated Bible Dictionary*. New York: Thames Nelson, 1988.

Meredith, J. L. *Meredith's Book of Bible Lists*. Minneapolis, Minnesota: Bethany House, 1980.

*New National Baptist Hymnal*. Nashville, Tennessee: National Baptist Publishing Board, 1977.

Spence, H. D. M., & Joseph S. Exell, eds. *The Pulpit Commentary*, vol. 9. Grand Rapids, Michigan: Wm. B. Eerdmans, 1974.

Vine, W. E., ed. *An Expository Dictionary of Biblical Words*. Nashville, Tennessee: Thomas Nelson, 1984.

*Webster's Seventh Collegiate Dictionary*. Springfield, Massachusetts: Merriam-Webster, 1972.

Young, Robert. *Young's Analytical Concordance to the Bible*. Nashville, Tennessee: Thomas Nelson, 1980.

**To contact Clarence Talley Sr., write:**

Clarence Talley Sr.
PO Box 2134
Prairie View, TX 77446-2134

www.clarencetalley.com

Printed in the United States
By Bookmasters